The Ultimate SAP® User Guide

REHAN ZAIDI

Published by JonERP.com

Paperback and Kindle versions available on Amazon.com

Published by eCruiting Alternatives, Inc. (JonERP.com)
Web site: JonERP.com

ISBN: 978-0-9725988-8-0
Available retail from Amazon.com
Available wholesale from Ingram

Copy Edit by Help Publish; Krista Wiebe
Style Review by Rachel Meyers
Cover Design & Interior Book Design by Magic Graphix

All of the product names in this book are trademarks of the companies that own them. SAP AG is the registered trademark holder of SAP, SAP R/3, ABAP, NetWeaver, SAP ERP, and other proprietary terms.

JonERP.com is not affiliated with SAP AG in any way. The technical information in this book has been verified to the greatest extent possible; however, any information found in this book is used at the reader's own risk.

JonERP.com reserves the right to correct any errors or omissions in any portion of this book at any time without obligation. While the author has done his best to present accurate and up to date technical information in this book, neither JonERP.com nor the author himself can guarantee that this information in this book is completely applicable to your company's SAP project. This book is sold with the understanding that the publisher and author are not engaged in rendering legal, accounting, or formal implementation services through this book. Should you want to confirm how this book's content applies to your company's project specifically, a paid consultation with the author is recommended.

Author's Acknowledgments

I would like to thank and dedicate this book to my mother – who is my main strength. I am very grateful to our editor Krista Wiebe of Clear Cut Editing (www.clearcutediting.com). She provided help with the overall editing, formation of the chapters, and provided layout suggestions. I am also thankful to Mr. Rick Porter (founder of Revelation Software, which is based in Australia) for his cooperation during this project. I am also indebted to the reviewers for helping me strengthen the content of the book. To all those who purchase this book - I am forever grateful to you. I would like to extend my apologies to anyone I have missed here.

Last but not least, I would like to thank my publisher, Jon Reed, who felt that this was a subject worth publishing and who agreed to go on this journey with me. The idea was to create a guide with tips and tricks that would be valuable for an SAP user. When I presented the idea to Jon, he agreed that the need for a user guide was an excellent reason to pursue the publication of my book.

Publisher's Acknowledgments

Jon Reed would like to thank Andy Klee of JDEtips for providing the basis for Jon and Rehan to originally meet and collaborate. The Ultimate SAP series would not be possible without the expert advice of Morris Rosenthal and Rachel Meyers. Thanks also to our expert readers, whose bios appear in the back of this book. Finally, Jon would like to thank Rehan Zaidi for his diligence and the outstanding end result.

Contents

Foreword

When I first met Rehan Zaidi, the author of the *Ultimate SAP User Guide*, he was still an aspiring writer. The year was 2003. As the Founding Editor of ERPtips, I was looking for writing talent. But that was not an easy thing to find, especially in the ERP world. I needed authors who had a deep SAP experience as well.

Rehan was already an expert SAP developer, user, and all-around HCM smart guy. Writing about SAP was new to him, but from his first articles, Rehan showed the ability to express complex and sometimes nerdy SAP concepts in ways readers could easily understand — something you will see on every page of this book.

It was a pleasure to edit Rehan's work. With each article, his ability to illustrate SAP concepts improved. Rehan was especially good at making sure that readers had takeaways from each article. You didn't have to read ten of his pieces to get something worthwhile. Each article had a stand-alone purpose.

The same is true of this User Guide. Each chapter has a clear objective for the reader. Whether it's Chapter 1 (SAP overview and basics), Chapter 4 (personalizing your SAP system), or Chapter 9 (creating your own reports), each chapter will give you something you can use immediately. *The Ultimate SAP User Guide* is a much more affordable alternative to a costly SAP training manual. You can also use it (or adapt it) for an instructor-led course, making it one of the more flexible SAP books out there.

I don't issue SAP books very often from JonERP.com. I rarely find an author with talent who can fill an important gap in the market. The last time around, JonERP published *The Ultimate SAP Pricing Guide* by SAP pricing expert Matthias Liebich. It's great to be adding to the "JonERP Ultimate" series with another book that I can be proud to share with the SAP community.

One thing about the JonERP Ultimate series: We don't publish 500 page encyclopedias. When we put out a book, we make sure it's easy to consume without weighing down your carry-on.

Over the years, I have heard from thousands of SAP professionals who are at some kind of crossroads in their SAP career. Even with the changes in the marketplace brought on by new technologies, many are eager to know if there are still chances in the SAP field.

What I tell them is that there are certainly opportunities, but despite what you might hear about SAP skills shortages, there's nothing easy about the SAP career path anymore. You have to develop an area of mastery and outperform your colleagues. But in a career paradox, you also need to be a team player. Shining at the expense of helping others out and being an expert AND a teacher is how you move ahead in today's SAP field.

Rehan has figured this out. The clues to his success can be found throughout this user guide. SAP professionals who want to excel — at any skill level — need to adopt a "continuous learning" mindset. To pull this off, you need to have the right reference tools handy. I believe this book can do that for you — otherwise I would not have published it. Publishing is far from easy, but it's an honor to get this book out there. I trust that you will get as much out of reading it as we did sharing it with you.

Jon Reed, JonERP.com

Introduction

This book is intended for all SAP users across every module, as well as beginners who are just starting out in the SAP world. If you are a new user, or if you have spent some time working on SAP, this book has a lot to offer. In addition, project team members and novice consultants may also find it useful.

This book will show users how to get the most out of their SAP system, and it will enable them to get their job done in as little time as possible. Even if you are an advanced user who works on SAP for hours each day, you will still find this book to be a valuable resource. There are many features (or newer options) of which even advanced users are not aware. There are plenty of lesser known tips and tricks, as well, that will help to broaden your knowledge of SAP. This book also provides more efficient ways of doing tasks that you carry out every day. We have made sure to update this book with the newest and less known GUI features, with which very few users are familiar.

The SAP User Guide is designed to be a one-stop resource to help you carry out day-to-day activities quickly and easily without the need to search for resources on the Internet or elsewhere. The chapters have been created in a goal-directed fashion, i.e., each chapter contains a number of sections, and each section is based on a task that may be performed or may be required by a user in their daily work.

Much of the information offered in the SAP world requires the typical user to scour the Internet for materials that pertain to his or her particular needs. That is not the case with this book. It is designed to be the handbook for the everyday user. Today's SAP user has a full plate of tasks and typically lacks the budget or time for classroom training. The goal of this book is to be an invaluable resource for a busy user who wants to stay on track — and on deadline.

You can use this book as a go-to-reference, or you can work your way through it like a training manual. If you choose to work your way through each chapter, by the end you should be very comfortable with the ideas, and it should enable you to work more efficiently and quickly within SAP. You will be able to work very comfortably within your functional area and carry out all facets of work, getting the most out of the SAP system, and availing the investment of your company. You will be a master of all commonly used SAP functions, whether they are related to data entry, reporting, or emailing options.

This book is comprised of twelve chapters. Here's a brief review of each one:

Chapter 1 - SAP Overview and Basics

This chapter will focus on basic SAP concepts, including transactions, menu items, and accessing Help screens.

Chapter 2 - Organizing Your Work Using Favorites

Favorites lets you save time by eliminating the need to search for frequently used transactions. Topics such as how to create Favorites for transactions, how to create folders, and how to download and upload Favorites will be covered.

Chapter 3 - Entering Data Into SAP

Entering Data into the SAP system is the most important job of any user. This chapter will outline how to enter data efficiently and effectively.

Chapter 4 - Personalizing – Changing SAP Look and Feel

This chapter will detail how to personalize your SAP system according to your unique preferences.

Chapter 5 - Executing Report Transactions and Downloading Output

This chapter gets you up to speed on the crucial topic of reporting. Functions covered in this chapter include how you can execute report transactions and download output.

Chapter 6 - Mastering Selection Screens

Selection Screens are an important element of the SAP system, and this chapter will cover the various ways you can make them more efficient and useful.

Chapter 7 - ALV Displays

The two types of ALV displays along with ALV lists and grids will be covered in this chapter.

Chapter 8 - Printing Guide

This chapter will introduce you to the printing options available within the various screen sets. Topics such as how to print window contents and how to convert spool requests to PDFs will be covered.

Chapter 9 - Creating Your Own Reports

SAP Query allows you to generate reports based on your own data and particular needs. This will be the main focus of this chapter.

Chapter 10 - SAP Business Workplace
Part 1 - Managing Documents

The primary emphasis of this chapter will be on how to manage documents within the SAP Business Workplace. Topics such as Transaction SBWP, how to use attachments, and how to forward documents will be covered.

Chapter 11 - SAP Business Workplace
Part 2 - Managing Workplace Items

This chapter will focus on working with Workplace and items within the SAP Business Workplace.

Chapter 12 - Miscellaneous Topics (and Helpful Tips)

Miscellaneous topics, such as displaying authorization check, object services, and attachment lists will be covered in this chapter.

If you are completely new to SAP, we suggest that you read the chapters sequentially (starting from chapter 1). Reading it straight through will offer the best experience for a beginner and will provide you with all the information you need that pertains to typical things that you may encounter within the SAP ERP landscape.

If you already have experience working in SAP, you may find it more helpful to skip to chapters that are relevant to your needs. This book can also be used for training users, both beginners and experienced, and for all modules of the SAP ERP system.

This compact volume is packed with valuable tips and tricks that outline the day-to-day activities a typical user will come across. Because of the array of gathered information in this one book, project teams should be able to save time and money by using it for training purposes. No single SAP training course contains the information found within this book.

This book is comprised of solely original content that has not been published elsewhere. It has been written with Windows users in mind. The screen shots are taken from ERP 6.0, Enhancement Pack 6. The latest version of SAP GUI (7.30) has been used in the preparation of the book. Most of the concepts are applicable for other SAP system releases. The information in this book holds true irrespective of the database used in the backend.

We hope this user guide will help you to be more productive on your project, in your daily work, and will advance your SAP career.

Chapter 1

SAP Overview and Basics

In order to use SAP effectively and efficiently, users and beginners need to understand some basic concepts and terminologies. This chapter will introduce you to those concepts and will provide an introductory overview of the topics that will be covered in detail later in the book. It will also briefly cover the typical work an SAP user may be expected to do.

This chapter will cover the following important topics:

- *Getting started with the basic SAP concepts*
- *User tasks and transaction concepts*
- *Managing sessions*
- *Transactions and menu items*
- *Accessing Help screens and other screen fields*

Some questions that will be answered in this chapter include:

- *How do I log in to the SAP system?*
- *What tasks will I be expected to perform as an SAP user?*
- *What are the typical components of the initial SAP screen?*
- *What is a transaction code?*
- *How do I search for a particular item or transaction in the SAP Easy Access Menu?*

Throughout the chapter, there will be examples and screenshots to help you understand the process of beginning your work in SAP. In this chapter, the terms **Window** and **Screen** will be used interchangeably.

1.1 Getting Started

In this section, we will learn how to get started with SAP. The first step is to log in to the intended SAP system. We will see in detail the steps that are required to log in to the system and the various options available on the login screen.

To log in to any SAP system, you will need to access the **SAP Logon Pad**. There are a number of ways to do this:

- From the Start menu, choose the *SAP Logon* program to launch the SAP Logon Pad as shown in Figure 1.1.

Figure 1.1: SAP Logon Pad Shortcut

- Alternately, you may choose the shortcut placed on your desktop as shown in Figure 1.2.

Figure 1.2: SAP Logon Desktop Shortcut

NOTE: The **SAP Logon Pad** is a Windows program that lets you log on to an SAP system by choosing from a displayed list of available systems. User may also modify this list according to their requirements.

This action will launch the SAP Logon Pad showing the list of systems into which you may log in (under *Connections* shown in Figure 1.3).

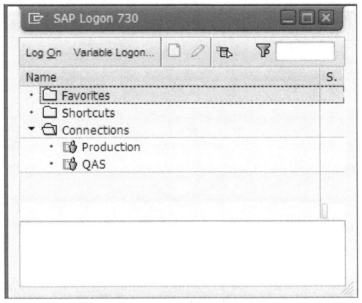

Figure 1.3: List of SAP Systems

Double-click the system that you wish to access. This will launch the screen as shown in Figure 1.4.

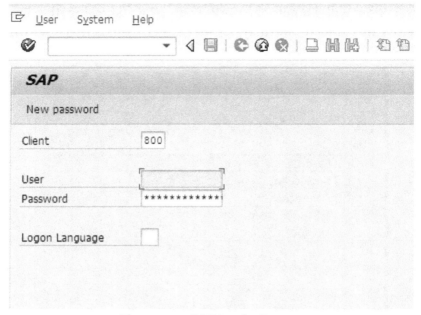

Figure 1.4: SAP Login Screen

The screen has *User* and *Password* fields, as well as *Client* and *Logon Language* fields. We also have at the top a menu and standard toolbar. (We will discuss these elements in the next section.)

Enter your user name and password in the appropriate fields on the login screen. Note that the system provides a default value for the client. In case you want a different client from the default shown, enter the new client's three-digit number in the field provided.

The language is an optional field. In our case, for example, the default system language is E (English). If you wish to enter a language other than the default language, you may also do that using the field provided.

Once the necessary data has been entered in the login screen, press "Enter" to log in to the system. Alternately, you may also click the green tick mark ✅ provided on the top left corner of the screen.

If you are logging in for the first time or if the security team has refreshed your password, you will be asked to enter a new password. Enter the new password twice and press "Enter" in the dialog box that appears.

To change a password while logging in, enter your existing User ID and Password but do not press "Enter". Rather, click the New password button. The system will ask for the new password and a confirmation.

If the password is initially entered incorrectly but then you finally succeed in logging in to the system, a dialog box (see Figure 1.5) appears showing the total *Number of failed logon attempts*.

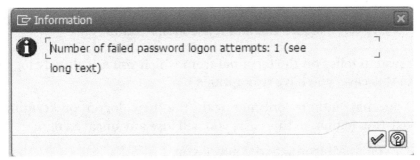

Figure 1.5: Number of Failed Attempts

If you have forgotten your password, you may ask the Security team members to refresh the password for your User ID. After six consecutive failed login attempts, your User ID will be locked and you may no longer be able to attempt logons into the system. In this case, you must ask the Security team members to unlock your User ID.

A user may attempt to log in more than once to the same system. In case you to want to log in to a system in which you are already logged in, a dialog box is shown (Figure 1.6) after the User ID and Password have been validated.

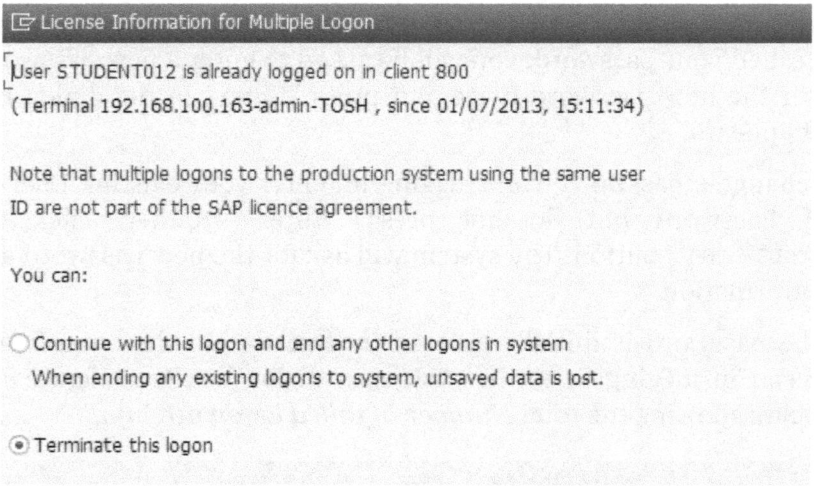

Figure 1.6: Multiple Logon Attempt

The system tells you the terminal from which you are already logged in. In this case, you have two options:

- You may either continue with the new logon or terminate existing logins. In this case, you will lose any unsaved data.

- Or you may terminate the new logon.

In some cases, a third option (not shown in Figure 1.6) may also appear which may allow you to proceed with the new logon as well as keeping the existing logons alive.

1.2 Basic Concepts - Initial Screen, Standard and User Menus

In this section, we will see how the SAP Initial screen looks, and we will also cover some basic SAP concepts necessary for users.

Once you have successfully logged in to the SAP system, the Initial **SAP Easy Access** screen is displayed, as illustrated in Figure 1.7. (The window shown in the figure is also sometimes referred to as a **Session**.)

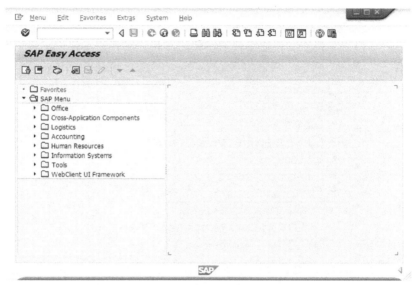

Figure 1.7: Initial SAP Screen

On the initial screen, either the **Standard Menu** or the **User Menu** will be displayed in the left side of the screen. In the previous figure, the left pane displays the SAP Easy Access Menu. It is in the form of a tree, which is comprised of nodes and subnodes. These allow you to access the programs within the relevant functional areas.

Clicking the black triangle ▸ next to the folder icon in the menu tree expands that node. (Alternately, you may double-click the given node icon.) This is illustrated in Figure 1.8 where the *Human Resources* node has been expanded.

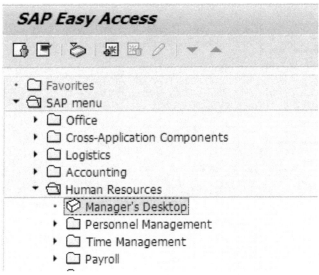

Figure 1.8: Navigating the Easy Access Menu

A node may contain additional nodes that can be expanded, such as *Personnel Management* and *Time Management* in Figure 1.8. Or a node may contain an executable application, such as *Manager's Desktop*. Note that these are indicated by the ⊘ icon. Double-click this item to execute the relevant application (transaction). In case a tree is already open, you may collapse it using the ▾ icon. You may navigate through the nodes (and their subnodes) until you reach the desired transaction.

Apart from the SAP standard menu shown in Figure 1.8, a user-specific **User Menu** is also defined in the system. The User *Menu* contains the reports and screens relevant to you or the ones that you use in your day-to-day work. For accessing the User Menu, choose the menu path *Menu → User Menu* as shown in Figure 1.9.

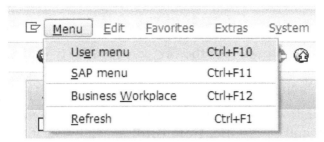

Figure 1.9: Accessing User and SAP Menu

> **NOTE:** In this section we only saw the *Menu* options. There are other useful options related to *Edit*, *Favorites,* and *Extras* menus. These will be discussed later in the book.

The user-specific menu is then displayed in the left pane as shown in Figure 1.10.

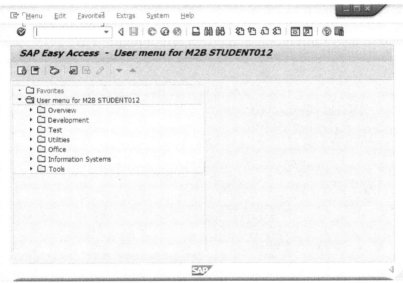

Figure 1.10: User-Specific Menu

1.3 SAP Window Components

In this section, we will see the components of a typical SAP screen. The concepts mentioned in this section pertain to all SAP screens in general, including the Initial Screen (mentioned in previous section).

An SAP Window consists of a **Menu Bar,** a **Standard Toolbar,** a **Title Bar,** and an **Application Toolbar**, all found at the top of the screen. The Standard Toolbar and Menu Bar together are known as the **Screen Banner**. These four components (Menu Bar, Application Bar, Standard Toolbar, and Title Bar) form the **Screen Header**.

Below the Screen Header is a larger portion called the **Screen Body**. Any screen that you display or any report you may execute is displayed in the Screen Body.

At the lower part of the screen is the **Status Bar** — important messages for the user (such as errors, information, and warnings) are displayed here. On the right side of the Status Bar is the relevant System and User information.

Consider, for example, the screen shown in Figure 1.11.

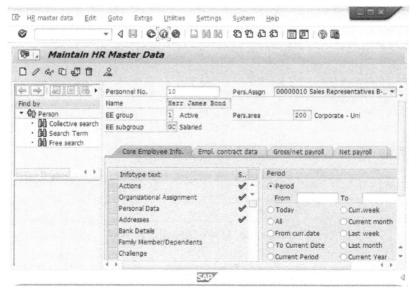

Figure 1.11: SAP Screen Components

Let us now have a closer look at the components of the screen shown in Figure 1.11:

- *Menu Bar*: You access the menu options in SAP just like you access the menus of typical Windows applications. If appropriately defined, the relevant menu options may be executed via keyboard shortcuts as well. The Menu Bar is context-sensitive and displays all options relevant to the screen being executed. For example, Figure 1.11 is the *Maintain Master Data* transaction and it includes the following menu options: *HR Master Data, Edit, Goto, Extra, Utilities, Settings, System,* and *Help.* Clicking on one of these menus results in a dropdown list of relevant options. For example, Figure 1.12 illustrates the options for the *HR Master Data* menu.

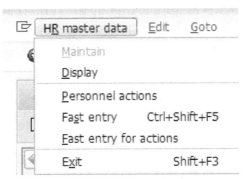

Figure 1.12: HR Master Data Options

Clicking on the displayed options will carry out the relevant activity.

In case a menu option consists of submenus, the submenu will be displayed when you place the cursor on the relevant menu item. For example, in the menu shown in Figure 1.13, when we place the cursor on the *Database Object* option, the additional options (*Display, Check,* and *Database Utility*) appear.

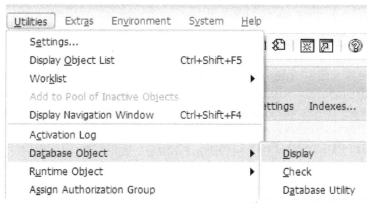

Figure 1.13: Menu Additional Options

- *Application Toolbar*: This is comprised of buttons and functions relevant to whatever application or program that you run. These change with the application programs. There may, for example, be additional detailed information buttons. The application toolbar for the HR Master Data screen is shown below:

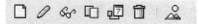

Figure 1.14: Application Toolbar for HR Master Data

- *Status Bar:* At the lower portion of the screen is the Status bar, which gives useful information to the user. The Status Bar consists of the Message area (on the left), which presents error messages or affirmative system messages, and the Status fields on the right. An example of a message is shown in Figure 1.15.

> ☑ Personnel number not yet assigned

Figure 1.15: Message in Status Bar

- *Standard Toolbar*: The Standard Toolbar is comprised of standard functions. These are generally provided in all SAP screens and applications that you run. However, some of the functions may be disabled, depending on the nature of the task being executed. The various functions of the Standard Toolbar are shown in Figure 1.16.

Icon	Meaning	Key Shortcut
✅	Enter	Enter key
💾	Save	CTRL+S
◀	Back	F3
⬆	Exit	Shift F3
❌	Cancel	F12
🖨	Print	CTRL+P
🔍	Search	CTRL+F
🔍	Search Again (or Continue Search)	CTRL+G
📄	First Page	CTRL Page UP
📄	Page Up	Page Up
📄	Page Down	Page Down
📄	Last Page	CTRL+Page DOWN
▦	Opens New Session	--
❓	Help	F1
🖥	Customize Local Layout	ALT+F12

Figure 1.16: Standard Toolbar Functions

On the top (left of the application toolbar) is the **Command Field** (Figure 1.17). This is an important field, as it lets you quickly access programs and screens.

Figure 1.17: Command Field

Simply entering the desired Transaction Code in this field will take you to the relevant program. This relieves the user from learning the menu path of the task that he or she wants to perform. (Refer to section 1.6 on how to use the Command Field for managing SAP sessions.)

1.3.1 Elements in Reports and Entry Screens

An SAP screen body may contain a number of screen elements. Typically, a screen contains input fields, output-only fields, radio buttons, and checkboxes for the purpose of entering data. This is applicable for all transactions — including data entry screens and reports.

If a field is grey (not white), it means that input is not allowed. It is mandatory to fill in the fields that appear with a question mark. This means that even if you try to move ahead of such screens, the error message, *Enter data in all required fields*, is displayed. Moreover, in data entry screens, to enter tabular data, multiple lines may be entered using a table.

A screen may also be comprised of tabstrips, consisting of a number of tabs. Each tab may contain a number of input and output fields, tables, as well as radio buttons and checkboxes. While processing of SAP screens, you may come across dialog boxes that may, for example, ask you for confirmation of an action. (For more information, refer to Chapters 3 and 6.)

For accessing the Help of a particular application, choose the menu path *Help → Application Help*. This will open the Help for that particular screen in a browser. To access the Help screen related to a particular field given on an SAP screen, simply place the cursor on the field and press F1. The Help will appear as shown in Figure 1.18.

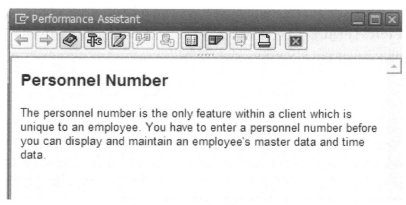

Figure 1.18: Field F1 Help

For viewing the technical information of the given field, click the *Technical Information* 📇 icon. The technical name of the field and other useful information will then be displayed.

1.3.2 System Status

Some useful information related to the system and your user ID is available from all SAP screens. To access this, click the *System →* *Status* button. This will display the status in a screen as shown in Figure 1.19.

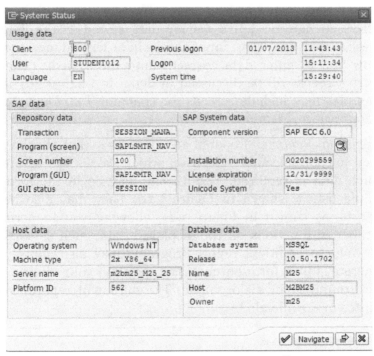

Figure 1.19: System Status Details

The Status box shows you information about the User ID, such as the Client, the User name, as well as the previous logon time, the time which you logged in, the current system time, and so on. On the same screen, there are details of the running Program and Transaction, as well as the machine on which the SAP server is running.

1.4 User Tasks

In this section, I will discuss the tasks that you may be expected to perform as an SAP user. In the SAP system, a task may comprise of one or more screens. Typically, you may come across the following tasks:

> **NOTE:** Tasks include completing process steps (such as creating an invoice or approving requests) or administrative tasks (such as checking messages). Furthermore, numerous reporting options are available to the user.

- *Data Entry*: This involves a set of screens that allow you to create, change, or delete display data stored in the database. These screens may have input checks in order and messages that allow you to enter data correctly into the system. (The Data Entry screens will be discussed in detail in Chapter 3.) Typical examples may include screens for changing *Employee Address* or for creating *Customer Master*.

- *Executing Reports*: Reports are programs that display data. They have a selection screen on which values are entered for which data is required. The display may be in the form of a simple list, as shown in Figure 1.20. They may also be ALV reports, as shown in Figure 1.21, allowing you to perform a number of functions on the displayed data, such as sorting or filtering. In addition, report programs may also allow you to generate simple form outputs. You may run your reports in the background or in dialog mode. The output of reports may be printed or downloaded.

Airline	Flight No.	Country	Depart. city	Depart	Country	Arrival city
AA	17	US	NEW YORK	JFK	US	SAN FRANCISCO
AA	64	US	SAN FRANCISCO	SFO	US	NEW YORK
AZ	555	IT	ROME	FCO	DE	FRANKFURT
AZ	788	IT	ROME	FCO	JP	TOKYO
AZ	789	JP	TOKYO	TYO	IT	ROME
AZ	790	IT	ROME	FCO	JP	OSAKA
DL	106	US	NEW YORK	JFK	DE	FRANKFURT
DL	1699	US	NEW YORK	JFK	US	SAN FRANCISCO

Figure 1.20: Simple List Output

ALV Object Model Solution

Carrier	Flight No.	Country Key	Depart. city	Dep. airport	Country
AA	17	US	NEW YORK	JFK	US
AA	64	US	SAN FRANCISCO	SFO	US
AZ	555	IT	ROME	FCO	DE
AZ	788	IT	ROME	FCO	JP
AZ	789	JP	TOKYO	TYO	IT
AZ	790	IT	ROME	FCO	JP
DL	106	US	NEW YORK	JFK	DE
DL	1699	US	NEW YORK	JFK	US

Figure 1.21: ALV Output

- *Other Tasks*: These may include completing process steps (such as execution of a payroll run, creating an invoice, or approval of travel requests). Furthermore, you may want to generate your own reports using SAP Query. Or you may come across useful transactions — such as the SAP Business Workplace — that will allow you to manage your work, check your SAP emails, or perform tasks such as approval of requests via Workflow items.

1.5 Transaction and Transaction Code

An important term that SAP users need to be familiar with is **Transaction**. Regardless of whether a user is executing tasks or generating reports, he or she does so via transactions, which is denoted by a code that is three or more characters long (comprising of letters and digits). These transactions may either be standard SAP transactions or custom defined ones.

Any task that you need to perform, either running a report or performing a particular activity, may be accessible either via the SAP Easy Access Menu shown in Figure 1.8, or via a shortcut known as a **Transaction code** (or sometimes called Tcode). For example, you have the standard transaction SBWP for accessing the SAP Business Workplace, or you may have an SAP report using Transaction code ZHRREP. You enter the Transaction code in the Command Field (and press "Enter") in order to quickly access a particular report or application screen. For example, we write the Transaction code "SBWP" in the Command Field for accessing the *Business Workplace* application as shown in Figure 1.22.

Figure 1.22: Transaction SBWP

NOTE: In order to access a particular report or screen transaction, the Security Team must provide your user ID with necessary authorizations.

Let us now see a few other examples of SAP transactions in various modules of the SAP system.

Within the *Materials Management* module, the user may maintain Materials via Transaction codes shown in Figure 1.23.

Transaction Code	Purpose
MM01	Create Material
MM02	Change Material
MM03	Display Material

Figure 1.23: MM Transaction Codes

The *Sales Order* is accessed via the transactions shown in Figure 1.24.

Transaction Code	Purpose
VA01	Create Sales Order
VA02	Change Sales Order
VA03	Display Sales Order

Figure 1.24: Sales Order Transaction Codes

For *Network Order*, the transactions are shown in Figure 1.25.

Transaction Code	Purpose
CN21	Create Network Orders
CN22	Change Network Orders
CN23	Display Network Orders

Figure 1.25: Network Order Transactions

1.5.1 Accessing Entered Transaction Codes Quickly

One quick way of going to a previously visited transaction (the code of which was entered in the Command Field) is by using the "Down" arrow key. The history of visited transactions may be viewed via the list box display of the Command Field. Suppose your field history looks like the one shown in Figure 1.26.

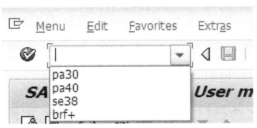

Figure 1.26: Command Field History

If you want to go directly to the BRF+ transaction, simply type "B" in the Command field (without opening the list display) and press the "Down" arrow key. The BRF+ transaction will appear in the Command Field. You may then simply press "Enter" to go to the BRF+ transaction.

Likewise, typing "P" or "PA" will display the PA30 and PA40 respectively. This will save you from having to type the entire PA30 or PA40 in the Command Field shown.

1.5.2 Searching for Transaction Codes (or Menu Items)

In case you want to search for a particular item or transaction in the SAP Easy Access Menu, you may do so using a standard SAP transaction. Follow the steps below:

- In the Command Field, enter the transaction "SEARCH_SAP_MENU". The dialog box appears as shown in Figure 1.27.

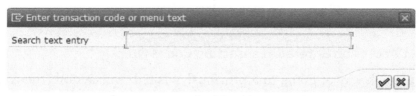

Figure 1.27: Searching Transaction

- Enter the text of the menu item or the text for the transaction that you want to search for and press the *(Continue/Enter)* button. The output will display the list of all menu items as well as their complete navigation path from the SAP access menu. Moreover, the relevant transaction code is also displayed. For example, the output of the Search program for the search text "Business Workplace" is shown in Figure 1.28.

Search for a Transaction Code or Menu Title

Node	Transaction code	Text
Nodes	SBWP	Business Workplace
Preceding node		Runtime tools
Preceding node		SAP Business Workflow
Preceding node		Development
Preceding node		ABAP Workbench
Preceding node		Tools
Nodes	SBWP	Business Workplace
Preceding node		Runtime tools
Preceding node		Development
Preceding node		Business Workflow
Preceding node		Tools

Figure 1.28: Searching "SAP Business Workplace"

1.6 Managing Sessions

In this section, we will see how to manage SAP Sessions. This includes a variety of ways to create new sessions, close existing sessions and log off from the SAP system.

You may create a new session or window from a running session by clicking the ⬚ icon (from the standard toolbar) or using the keyboard shortcut "CTRL+N". Multiple sessions will allow the user to work on more than one task at one time. A maximum of six sessions (windows) are allowed for one login. In case you try to create a session above this limit, the system will issue a message stating *Maximum Number of Sessions Reached.* You may switch between sessions using the "ALT+Tab" keys. There may be a number of sessions for a number of servers such as QAS and Production running on your machine. (The procedure for logging in to a particular system has been discussed in detail in the beginning of the chapter.)

There are a number of ways to close a session. A quick and easy way is to use the ⬚ icon at the top right corner of the window. This will close the session.

Another option is to use the *SAP Logon* ⬚ icon in the system tray. Right-clicking the icon will show the context menu as shown in Figure 1.29.

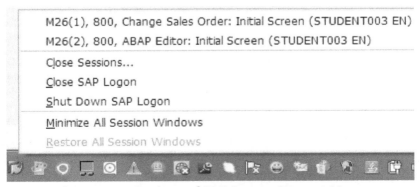

Figure 1.29: Options of SAP Logon Context Menu

This figure shows the various context menu options. On top, you will be shown the various SAP systems that you are logged in to. For example, in Figure 1.30, I am logged in to server M26, for client 800 by the user name STUDENT003, in the English language (EN). The number in the parentheses indicates the session number.

Two useful options available in the context menu are *Close Sessions* and *Shut Down SAP Logon.* Clicking the *Close Sessions* option displays a dialog box shown in Figure 1.30.

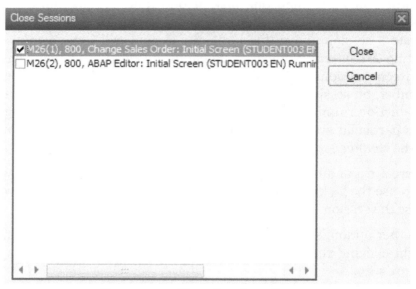

Figure 1.30: Close Sessions Screen

This shows all the currently running sessions along with the transaction you are executing. Select the checkbox for the session(s) that you want to close and then click the *Close* button. The selected session(s) will then be closed and any unsaved data will be lost.

In case you want to close all running sessions quickly, click the option *Shut Down SAP Logon* (shown in Figure 1.29). A message warning you of the loss of data upon termination of all sessions is displayed as shown in Figure 1.31.

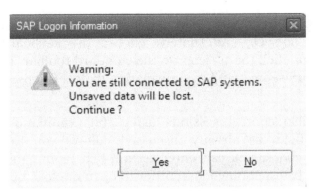

Figure 1.31: Closing All Sessions

Click the *Yes* button to terminate all the running sessions.

If a session is hanging and you would like to stop the transaction that was running in the session, simply click the ☞ icon at the top left corner of the session window. A menu will appear as shown in Figure 1.32.

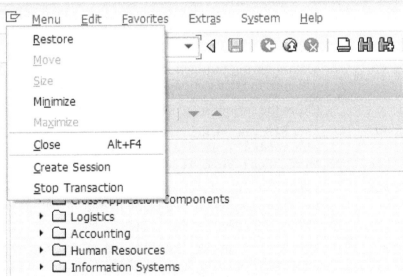

Figure 1.32: Menu to Stop Transaction

Choose the *Stop Transaction* option from this menu.

For logging off from an SAP system, simply choose the menu path *System* → *Log Off*. Alternately, choose the keyboard shortcut "Shift+F3" or click the 🔖 icon on the standard toolbar. In all cases, you will be presented with a confirmation dialog. Choose option *Yes* to proceed.

You may also control sessions using the Command field. The Command field, as already discussed, allows you to enter the transaction codes. You can enter certain text (commands) with or without the transaction code in order to open or close new sessions. Figure 1.33 shows the various inputs that can be made in the Command Field and the relevant system behavior.

Field Input	Purpose
/o	This opens a list of all running sessions and their transactions. You may end a session using the *End Session* button provided in the list dialog.
/n	This closes the current session.
/nex	Closes all sessions of currently connect system and logs you off. Any changes not saved will be lost.
/otcode	The '/o' followed by a transaction code will open a new session having transaction in it. For example, /oSBWP will open the transaction SBWP in a new session.
/n	Closes the current session and opens a new session.
/nend	This logs you off the system. In this case, however, a conformation message is displayed before the termination of sessions.
/ntcode	This input will take you to the transaction specified in the same session. If you want to return to the start menu, type '/ns000' in the Command Field.
/1,/2	This lets you quickly close the session denoted by the number followed by forward slash '/'. For example, if you type /1 in the Command Field, the first session will be closed.

Figure 1.33: Command Field Inputs

Summary of Chapter 1

Chapter 1 contains a lot of information about the basic concepts and terminology of SAP that users need to understand in order to use SAP effectively and efficiently.

Some of the topics that were covered in detail in this chapter include getting started with the basic SAP concepts, user tasks and transaction concepts, managing sessions, transactions and menu items, and accessing Help screens and other screen fields. These basic concepts are essential knowledge for users.

I hope this chapter has been a helpful guide to get you started to work in SAP. In the next chapter, we will use this knowledge to further study and understand SAP.

Chapter 2

Organizing Your Work Using Favorites

Chapter 1 covered how to get started with SAP, the logging in process, and the basics of the screens and session. In this chapter, we will discuss another important part of a user's life — organizing your work using Favorites. Favorites let you save time by eliminating the need to search for frequently used transactions.

This chapter will cover the following important topics:

- *What are Favorites?*
- *Creating Favorites for transactions*
- *Creating Favorites from user menu items*
- *Creating a Favorite while being in a transaction*
- *Creating Folders*
- *Downloading and Uploading Favorites*

This chapter will describe a number of ways to add Favorites and organize your work. It will begin with a brief overview of what Favorites are and how to utilize them effectively. After the overview, we will dive into the various ways in which you can create Favorites and how to organize them with folders.

Because users mostly use transactions, I will also focus on how to add or delete transactions from Favorites. Some questions answered in this chapter include:

- *How can I create a Favorite for my transaction?*
- *How can I organize my list of Favorites?*
- *Can I delete a Favorite once it has been created?*

Throughout the chapter, there will be examples and screenshots to help the reader understand the process of creating and organizing Favorites.

2.1 What are Favorites?

SAP allows users to save their frequently used program or transaction names as **Favorites** in their personalized menu tree (see Figure 2.1). This transaction can be executed by simply double-clicking on the relevant *Favorite* node. This will save you time as well as relieve you from remembering lengthy transaction codes.

The menu pertaining to Favorites (as seen from the Initial screen) is shown in Figure 2.1. The menu contains useful features, such as creating Favorite nodes, creating folders for Favorites, as well as downloading and uploading them to and from your local PC.

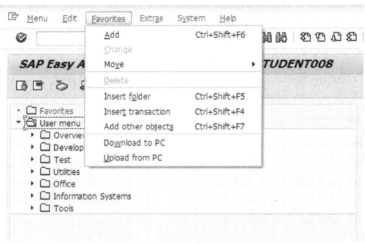

Figure 2.1: Menu Path for Favorites

Alternately, you may use the initial screen toolbar that has been made for this purpose, as seen in Figure 2.2.

Figure 2.2: Related Toolbar Buttons

The *Delete* button will only be enabled if you have at least one item under your *Favorites* node. Otherwise, the *Delete* 📇 button will not be enabled.

2.1.1 Adding to the Favorites Node

Right-click on the *Favorites* node from the *SAP Easy Access Menu*. The context menu appears as shown in Figure 2.3.

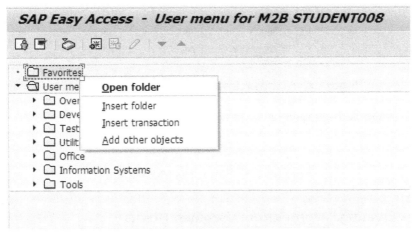

Figure 2.3: Context Menu of the Favorites Node

Choose the *Insert Transaction* option. The pop-up box for entering the Transaction Code appears as shown in Figure 2.4.

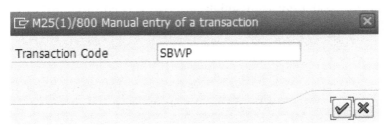

Figure 2.4: Entering the Transaction Code

Enter the Transaction Code in the field provided, e.g., "SBWP" for Business Workplace, and press "Enter". This creates a shortcut to the transaction, in our case, *Business Workplace* under *Favorites* (see Figure 2.5).

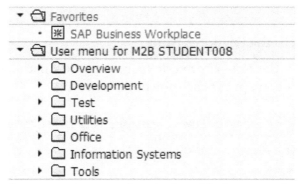

Figure 2.5: Transaction Code Added as Favorite

A message is displayed as shown.

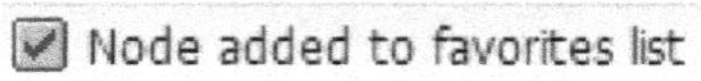

Figure 2.6: Favorites Message

2.1.2 Creating Favorites from User Menu Items

Another quick and easy way for creating Favorites of your transactions listed in the SAP Easy Access Menu is to select the given node and click the ![button] button.

Alternately, you may right-click, choose the context menu option, and then choose the option *Add to Favorites* (see Figure 2.7).

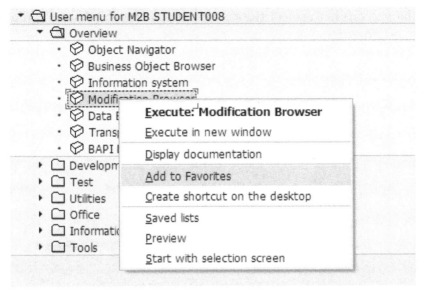

Figure 2.7: Context menu for adding a Favorite

You may also use keys "CTRL+Shift+F6" instead of the menu path.

The selected transaction may be added to your Favorites via drag and drop. Simply select a given transaction node from your *User* menu and then, while keeping the mouse button pressed, drag the item to the relevant position under the *Favorites* node or its folder or subfolder. Then release the mouse button.

In all cases, a successful message will appear saying *Node Added to Favorite List*.

For checking the functioning of your Favorite, simply double-click on the relevant node. The relevant transaction will be displayed.

2.1.3 Creating a Favorite While Being in a Transaction

All of the above techniques work when you are on the Initial screen of SAP. Suppose you are "on" a transaction that you would like to add as a Favorite. The simplest way (without the need to type the Transaction Code in the Command Field and/or going back to the

Initial screen) is to select the menu path *System → User Profile →
Expand Favorites.*

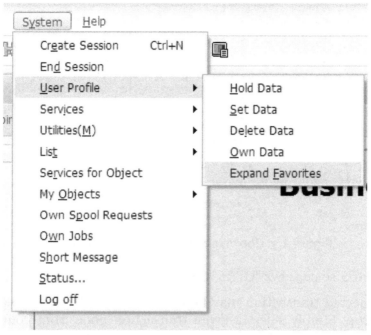

Figure 2.8: Menu Path for Creating a Favorite from a Transaction

TIP: If you are within a transaction and the SAP can be easily
accessed, then you use the menu option *System → User Profile
→ Expand Favorites.* This is useful, as you don't need to go back
to the Initial SAP screen.

2.2 Creating Folders

When you have a number of Favorite items added, the list might
become very large and confusing. To better organize the list, you
may create folders and subfolders within your Favorites and place
new Favorites within them.

In this section, we will cover how to create folders and subfolders for our Favorites, thus making our work more organized.

To create a folder, select the Favorites node and right-click in order to access the context menu. Next, choose the menu option *Insert Folder*.

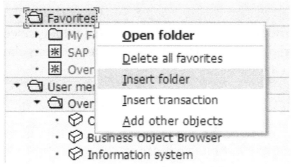

Figure 2.9: Creating a Folder

A dialog box appears as shown in Figure 2.10.

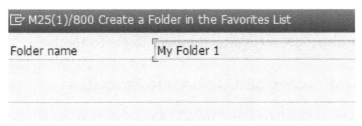

Figure 2.10: Folder Name

Enter a suitable name for the folder and then press "Enter". A new folder will be created by the name specified.

We may create folders within the new folder by using the same context menu option. Transactions may be added to the folders using the steps listed in the previous section.

2.3 Deleting Favorites and Displacing Favorites

You may also delete Favorites or change their position from within the various folders.

For deleting Favorite nodes, select the relevant node and click the 🔳 button. The Favorite will be removed from the *Favorites* list.

> **NOTE:** For deleting all Favorites within a folder, select the given folder and right-click to access context menu. Then choose option "Delete All Favorites".

To change the sequence of existing Favorites, follow these steps:

- Select the node of the Favorite whose position is to be changed by pressing the left mouse button.

- While keeping the left mouse button pressed, move the cursor to the new (desired) position.

- Then release the left mouse button. This places the Favorite into the new position.

You may also move a Favorite from one folder to another.

2.4 Downloading and Uploading Favorites

You may also download and upload Favorites that have been added to your personalized menu. This is particularly useful when you, for example, have all of your Favorites in one system, such as QA system, and you want to transfer them to another system, for example, Production. You may simply download from one and upload to another without wasting your time creating the entire set of Favorite folders from scratch.

To download Favorites on the local PC, proceed as follows:

- In the SAP Easy Access Menu, choose the menu path *Favorites → Download to PC* (see Figure 2.11).

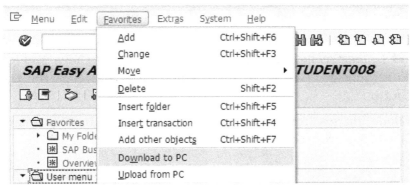

Figure 2.11: Menu Path "Download to PC"

- The dialog box appears as shown in Figure 2.12.

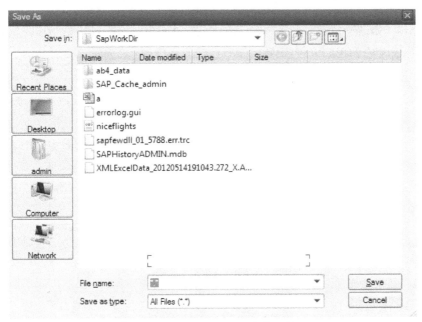

Figure 2.12: Save As Dialog Box

Enter a suitable file name after navigating to an appropriate location, and click the *Save* button. This will save the Favorites and their folders on your local PC at the given location.

To upload the saved Favorites from the desktop, proceed as follows:

- In the SAP Easy Access Menu, choose the menu path *Favorites → Upload from PC*. A dialog box similar to that shown in Figure 2.12 appears. Choose a suitable file name and click the *Open* button.

  Node entries from the selected file are read, and the relevant Favorites are created in the system.

Summary of Chapter 2

This chapter outlines how to create and effectively use Favorites. With the information provided, you should now be able to explain what they are and how to create them. You should also be able to create folders and organize your Favorites list, as well as download and upload your Favorites.

Chapter 3

Entering Data Into SAP

The most important part in the day of any user is the entry of data into the SAP system. In this chapter we will cover this process, including the typical entry screens, their various components, and their behavior on screen. This chapter will cover the following important topics:

- *Data Entry Transactions/Screens*
- *Value Help (Search Help) for Input Fields*
- *Copying Multiple Values From Screen With "CTRL+Y"*
- *Defining Default Values for an Input Field*
- *Hold Data and Set Data Functionality*
- *Object Manager*

By learning how to efficiently input data into the SAP system, you will save time in your everyday work life and your work will become more organized and easier to access. Some questions that will be answered in this chapter include:

- *What does a Data Entry Transaction look like?*
- *How can I create a Variant for Object Manager?*
- *How can I effectively use an F4 Help Hit List?*

Throughout the chapter, there will be examples and screenshots to help the reader gain the greatest possible understanding of how to effectively enter data into the SAP system.

3.1 Data Entry Transactions and Screens

Data is entered into the SAP system using data entry transactions. You may execute these transactions from a transaction code or an SAP easy access/user access menu path.

An **Entry Transaction** may consist of a number of screens. The user may enter data on one screen and may be required to go to a number of other screens while completing the data entry sequence. Each screen may contain validations and checks (required for consistency of data) that may generate error or warning messages.

SAP views all entities (items) whose data is to be maintained as **Objects**. Typical examples of objects are Sales Order, Notification, and Employee. As already mentioned in Chapter 1, there may be different transactions that Create, Change, and Display these objects.

> **NOTE:** Separate transactions are provided for Creation, Change, and Display for objects, each of which is denoted by a different transaction code. This was discussed in Chapter 1.

Before you are taken to the actual data entry screen(s), each transaction, whether pertaining to creation or change of objects, takes you to an *Initial Screen*. The Initial screen for Create transactions is different from those of Change and Display transactions. For example, on the Sales Order Creation Initial screen, there are fields such as *Order Type, Sales Organization*, and *Distribution Channel*, as shown in Figure 3.1.

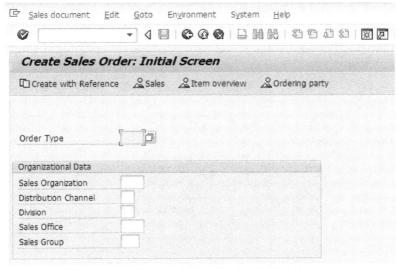

Figure 3.1: Create Sales Order Initial Screen

On the *Sales Order Change: Initial Screen*, for example, we have the *Order Number* (in this case the "object" under consideration) and other Search Criteria, such as *Billing Document* and *Sold-to-party*. After entering the object number on the initial screen, you will be taken to the actual data entry screen. For example, the main SD Change Order screen is shown in Figure 3.2.

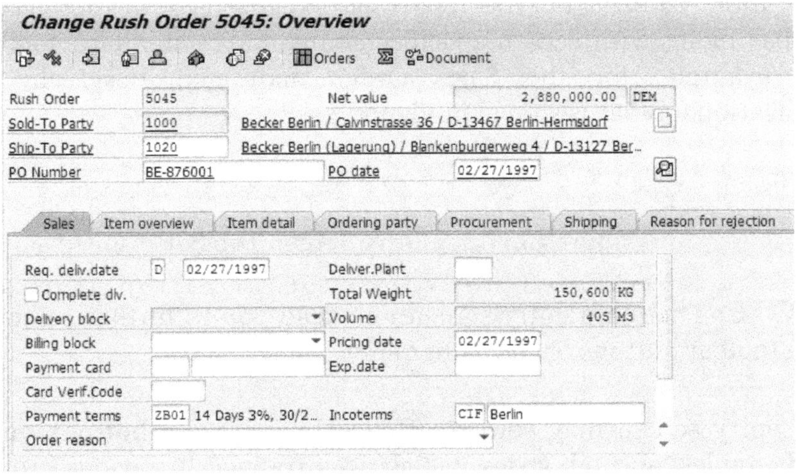

Figure 3.2: SD Data Entry Screen

Similarly, a typical data entry screen for HR is shown in Figure 3.3.

Change Personal Data

Pers. No.	88838	Pers.Assgn	00088838 00088838 Technicians ... ▾
Name	Mr. Danika Aahan		
	Atlanta	Active	
	Atlanta	Hourly rate/staff	No Payroll
Start	01/01/1970 ☐ To	12/31/9999	Chng 04/22/2009 I041477

Name

Title	1 Mr. ▾	Name Format	
Last name	Aahan	Birth name	
First name	Danika	Second name	
Middle name		Initials	
Second title	▾	Nickname	
Suffix	▾		
Name	Mr. Danika Aahan		

HR data

SSN	123-12-3212	Gender	
Birth date	01/01/1970	○ Female ◉ Male ○ TBD	
Language	EN English ▾		
Nationality	▾	Other nat.	▾ ▾
Mar. Status	▾ Since	No. chld.	

Figure 3.3: Personal Data Entry Screen

The initial screen and the following screens have an application toolbar along with screen-specific menus and a standard toolbar. For example, for the Sales Order maintenance screen, the application toolbar is shown in Figure 3.4.

Figure 3.4: Data Entry Screen Toolbar

> **NOTE:** The main entry screen may lead you to further screens via toolbar buttons or the *Goto* menu.

The entry screen may consist of checkboxes, radio buttons, input fields, tables, and tab strips, which are arranged in various groups. Let us discuss some of the important elements one by one:

- *Input fields.* These allow for the entry of data and appear editable (white-colored). The input fields can be of various sizes and types. Typical examples include Date Input field, Amount, or a Text or Code Input field. Additional text may be displayed when a particular set of data is entered in a field and then "Enter" is pressed. For example, if we enter "01" in the *Personnel Subarea (PS Area)* field, the text *Philadelphia* is displayed next to it.

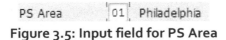

Figure 3.5: Input field for PS Area

You may use the F4 search help in order to find out the possible set of values applicable for entry in a given input field (this is discussed in the next section). An input field may be either mandatory or optional. A mandatory field, if left empty, will not allow you to go to the next screen or even to another tab. The mandatory field appears with a tick mark as shown in Figure 3.6.

Figure 3.6: Mandatory Field On Screen

For input fields, the **AutoCompletion** option is also supported. This means that when you enter a value in a field, input help in the form of Auto Completion is available from the previous set of entered values as shown in Figure 3.7.

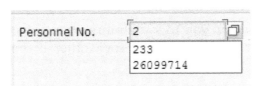

Figure 3.7: AutoCompletion

NOTE: When entering data into an input field, use "Backspace" to see the previously entered set of values. These are AutoCompletion values, and are system independent.

- *Dropdown List.* The Dropdown list is used for displaying a number of options in a list box and the user can choose one from the list, such as the one shown in Figure 4.8. By default, only the description is displayed and is available for selection. Settings may be applied in order to display the codes as well as the description of the field in question.

Address type	1 Permanent residence	▼
Care Of	4 Emergency address	
Address line 1	3 Home address	
	7 Home address acc. to contract	
Address line 2	R2 Hotel accomodation provided by employer	
City/county	90 Hukou address-CN	
	5 Mailing address	
State/zip code	6 Nursing address	
Country Key	US01 Paycheck Location	
Telephone Number	1 Permanent residence	▲
	2 Temporary residence	▼

Figure 3.8: Dropdown List

- *Checkboxes.* These are indicators as shown in Figure 3.9.

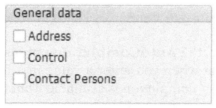

General data

☐ Address
☐ Control
☐ Contact Persons

Figure 3.9: Checkboxes on a Screen

Checkboxes allow you to switch an option (or condition) on or off. These are independent of each other if there are multiple checkboxes on a screen.

- *Radio buttons.* These are elements that allow you to choose one option from a number of options. They may be arranged horizontally or vertically. Within a group you may choose one radio button only.

Figure 3.10: Radio buttons

- *Buttons*. Buttons may take you to another screen or display further information. They may be displayed either with or without icons as shown in Figure 3.11 and Figure 3.12 respectively.

Figure 3.11: Button without Icon

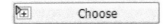

Figure 3.12: Button with Icon

In certain screens, there may also be expandable buttons that allow you to hide or show a set of elements on the screen.

- *Tables*. The table is an important element of the data entry screen. A typical table for entering data is shown in Figure 3.13.

Wage Type Long Text	Amount	Currency	
Monthly salary	5,167.00	EUR	
		EUR	
		EUR	

Figure 3.13: Data Entry Table

Each line lets you enter data. For example, a list of salary components may look like the one shown. Depending on the setting, Single or Multiple lines may be selected. Each line may have checkbox, input fields, or display fields.

NOTE: You may alter certain settings of the table (such as changing the sequence of displayed fields) to meet your needs. This is known as **Table Configuration**. They may be stored and accessed later.

To alter the table settings, first make any changes in the table look. For example, you may change the sequence of the table fields. To do this, simply drag the fields by selecting the column header and then place them in the position of your choice. For storing the configuration, click on the ⅲ icon on the top right corner of the table. This will display the *Table Settings* dialog shown in Figure 3.14.

Figure 3.14: Table Settings

The changes to the table settings may be stored in the form of Variants. Enter a suitable name for your variant in the field provided and then click the *Create* button. This will create the variant. Press the *Save* button. The next time that you access the table settings, you may choose the variant that you have just created in order to display the table in the changed format.

- *Tabstrips.* These are used in order to accommodate multiple sub-screens within a given area on the main screen. A typical tabstrip that may be displayed is shown in Figure 3.15.

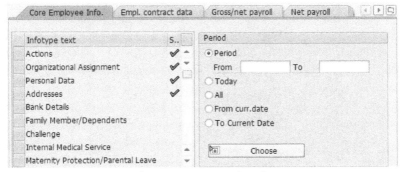

Figure 3.15: A Tabstrip

Each sub-screen may be accessed by clicking the relevant tab that may contain its own elements such as input fields, checkbox, tables, and so on. When a certain tab is clicked, it becomes active and the various components on it are shown.

You may also use the ◄ and ► icons to move left and right respectively. This is helpful in case there are many tabs that are not all visible on the screen. Alternatively, you may click the 🗔 icon on the upper right of the tabstrip in order to display the various tab names in the form of a menu as shown in Figure 3.16.

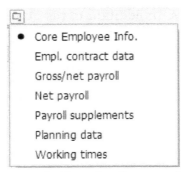

Figure 3.16: Choosing from a tab list

You may then choose the tab you need.

- *Context Menus.* Apart from the screen elements listed above, there are also context menus that can be used for a screen field or table field. Right-clicking a particular field will display a context menu from which further tasks may be chosen as shown in Figure 3.17.

Help	F1
Choose	F2
Back	F3
Possible Entries	F4
Create	F5
Change	F6
Display	F7
Cancel	F12
Delimit	Shift+F1
Delete	Shift+F2
Exit	Shift+F3
Overview	Shift+F8
Copy	Shift+F9
Lock/Unlock	Shift+F12
Fast entry	Ctrl+Shift+F5

Figure 3.17: Context Menu

- *Long Text Editors.* In addition to the above, a few screens may also allow you to enter long text using a long text editor as shown in Figure 3.18. This may either be accessible from a menu path or a button shown on the main entry screen.

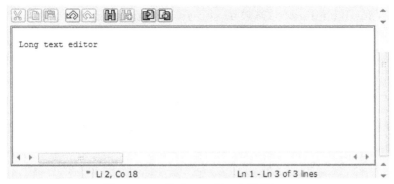

Figure 3.18: Long Text Editors

3.2 Entering Data on Screens

When you enter input on any of the screen fields and then press "Enter", the entered texts (such as names) are made left-justified, whereas the amount, number, and quantity fields are automatically made right-justified by the system.

After entering data in a particular field, you may press the "Tab" key to go on to the next field. There are tab sequences defined for each screen that specifies the sequence of input fields in which the cursor is placed by the system each time the tab button is pressed. If you do not want to use the Tab key, you may select a field using the mouse.

By default, the **Insert** mode is on for data entry. This means that when the cursor is on a field, entering any data will insert value in the field and will not overwrite the existing values. When a field is selected using the mouse, you may overwrite the old value in the field by switching on the **Overwrite** mode. This may be done by pressing the INS key once. Alternately, you may press the INS shown in the right part of the status bar as shown in Figure 3.19.

Figure 3.19: Insert Mode On

The INS will change to *OVR* as shown in Figure 3.20.

Figure 3.20: Overwrite Mode On

NOTE: The newest GUI allows you to edit the sequence of the tabs for the various input fields.

Simple Cut and Copy functions work for single input fields when entering data. For multiple field data selection and copy, we use the "CTRL+Y" keys. This is discussed ahead in section 3.4 of this chapter - Copying Multiple Values from Screen with "CTRL+Y".

When an entry is made on the screen and the "Enter" button is pressed, any validation checks are run. You may see errors, warnings, or simply information messages depending on the scenario.

An error message with a red symbol within a status bar is shown in Figure 3.21.

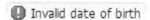

Figure 3.21: Error Message in Status Bar

An error will not allow you to proceed further with your data entry until the correct data is inputted. In the example shown, entering a valid date in the relevant field will not show the error any further and the user is allowed to proceed ahead. No saving of data is allowed if the error persists.

On the other hand, a warning appears as shown in Figure 3.22. The Warning symbol is yellow.

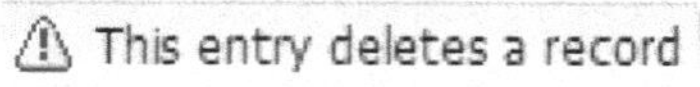

⚠ This entry deletes a record

Figure 3.22: Warning

This only warns the user that proceeding further will delete a record from the database. Pressing "Enter", for example, in such cases, will make the message disappear. The user may then be allowed to save data on the screen.

Instead of the status bar, messages may be displayed in dialog boxes depending on your personalized settings (we will see this in Chapter 4 - Changing SAP Look and Feel).

Also of importance are some of the standard toolbar buttons and icons used. These are *Save, Cancel,* and *Back*. The icons of the Cancel, Exit, and Back buttons are shown in Figure 3.23.

Button	**Icon**
Exit	⬆️
Back	⬅️
Cancel	❌

Figure 3.23: Cancel, Exit, and Back Buttons

The three buttons look similar in functioning, however, their working differs. When you want to come out of a transaction without saving, you may simply cancel the transaction by pressing the *Cancel* button. This will give you a prompt that says, *Do you want to Cancel?* If you want to stay on the transaction, press *No.* Otherwise, choose *Yes.* In this case, no option to save the data is presented to the user.

Suppose the user is editing an object that is comprised of header data as well as some other groups of data, each of which are entered on separate screens. If the user accesses only some of the screens, and after finishing data entry for a particular group he or she returns to the main entry screen, it is done via the *Back* button. If the *Back* button is pressed without saving the data on a particular screen, a dialog box is shown to the user warning him or her of possible loss of data. If the *Yes* option is chosen, the data is saved and the user is taken to the upper level in the application hierarchy.

The *Exit* button is used when the user, who has been entering data in an application, wants to leave (exit from) the application and move on to another task. When the *Exit* button is pressed, the system reminds him or her to save the entered data (if this is not done already).

For both *Back* and *Exit*, any data entry checks relevant to the screen are executed. For *Cancel*, no checks are executed for the data entered on the screen.

3.3 Value Help (Search Help) for Input Fields

In Chapter 1, we discussed the F1 - Field Help. You may refer back to that chapter for information on field help or for any information you require for particular input fields. In addition to the F1 help, an **Input Help** also known as F4 Help is available. In this section, we will see how to access the Value Help for input fields.

For accessing the Hit List, simply place the cursor on the field and then press the "F4" key. Alternately, after focusing on the field, press the small symbol □ displayed on the field's right side. This will display the Hit List as shown in Figure 3.24.

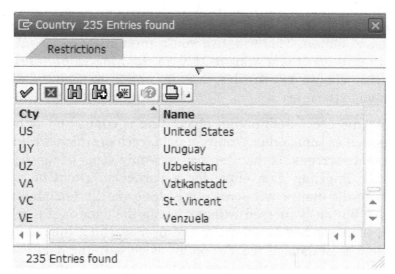

Figure 3.24: F4 Value Help

This allows you to see all possible sets of values (shown in the form of a Hit List) that may be entered in the field in question.

The value help provides various functions via the buttons in the available toolbar as shown in Figure 3.25.

Figure 3.25: Toolbar

You can sort the list according to a particular field in either ascending or descending order. This may be done by selecting a particular column or by choosing a column and then right-clicking in order to access the context menu. After this is done, choose the option *Sort Ascending* or *Descending* as shown in Figure 3.26.

Cty	Name
ZW	Zimbabwe
ZR	Zaire
ZM	
ZA	
YU	
YT	
YE	
WS	
WF	
VU	
VN	
VI	
VG	
VE	
VC	
VA	
UZ	
UY	
US	
UM	
UG	

Copy
Help
Create Values
Insert in Personal List
Sort in Ascending Order
Close
Personal Value List
Technical Info
Sort in Descending Order
Find
Find Again
Personalize
Delete Current Column
Select Current Column
Print Locally ▶
Print (Server)
Download

235 Entries found

3.26: Context Menu for Hit List

For an input field in which, for example, a code is to be entered, the input help will display the permissible codes and also their descriptions.

The Hit List may contain a very large number of values. You may filter the values based on the applicable criteria. For filtering the values, click the ▽ bar at the top of the list values. The fields for restricting the Hit List appear as shown in Figure 3.27.

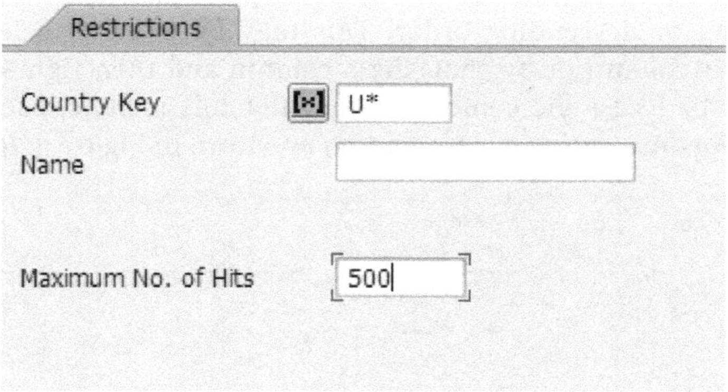

Figure 3.27: Filtering Values

Enter the appropriate values in the field provided to define your restriction criteria and then press "Enter".

For example, in the case of our country code and description, the default maximum number of hits is 500. We can change this to 6 and select only country codes beginning with 'U'. Then the Hit List will appear changed as shown in Figure 3.28.

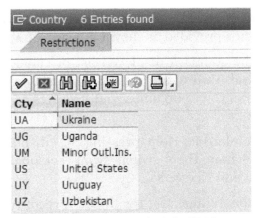

Figure 3.28: Restricted Hit List

The Help shown in Figure 3.24 and 3.28 is a simple search help. Other than that, you may also come across input help that is comprised of multiple tabs as shown in Figure 3.29. They are termed as **Collective Search Helps**.

Last name	First name	Title	Birth date	Pers.No.	Start Date
Rodolfo	Andres	Lic.	06/01/1963	00290004	06/01/1963
Vega	Adriana	Lic.	10/17/1975	00323200	10/17/1975
Mueller	Arturo	Ing.	01/01/1960	00009911	01/01/1960
Weijden	Hugo	Drs.	02/14/1974	00004000	02/14/1974
Perez Moreno	Sandra	Dr.Math.	05/20/1969	00290015	05/20/1969
Braunstein	Herbert	Dr.	11/16/1938	00001009	11/16/1938
Browning	Johanna	Dr.	02/26/1953	00001026	02/26/1953
Carbajal	Atilio	Dr.	06/14/1960	00290022	06/14/1960
Centeno	Rolando	Dr.	05/30/1955	00290016	05/30/1955
Chef	Heinz	Dr.	05/23/1940	00001907	05/23/1940
Copy of Last ...	Copy of Frst ...	Dr.	11/16/1938	00011247	11/16/1938
Jost	Martin	Dr.	05/14/1948	00001027	05/14/1948
Kuhl-Mayer	Henriette	Dr.	06/12/1958	00001950	06/12/1958
Maldonado	Roberto	Dr.	04/04/1948	00290024	06/03/1970

Personnel Number (1) 5000 Entries found

Last name - First name   Person ID   Person...

5000 Entries found

Figure 3.29: Collective Search Help

In this case, the relevant tab may be selected and input values entered in the fields provided as shown in Figure 3.29.

In addition to the standard displayed list of values, you may also create a **Personal Value List** (a set of values for yourself). This personal list allows you to organize your favorites or your frequently accessed values.

Instead of the standard F4 Help, pressing "F4" displays the Personal Value List. You may then switch from Personal Value list to standard Hit List and vice versa.

To create a Personal Value List (or to add a record into a Personal Value List) select a row from the standard Hit List and then click the ⊞ button on the toolbar. This will add the value to the Personal Value List and will create the list if it does not exist already. To view the Personal Value list, click the ⓘ button.

> **NOTE:** You may also create Personal Value Lists along with the standard F4 Help. A personal list, as the name denotes, is a list of values that you have personally chosen. It will be shown rather than the default search help list.

Once values are entered in the Personal Value List, accessing the F4 Help next time for the field in question will display the Personal Value List rather than the standard help list. You may switch back to the standard list by clicking the *Display All Values* 🔘 button in the toolbar.

3.4 Copying Multiple Values from Screen with "CTRL+Y"

A useful function provided by all SAP screens is the facility to copy multiple values from a set of input fields or table lines at one time using the "CTRL+Y" keys. To do this, follow the steps below:

- First, press the "CTRL+Y" keys. Alternately, you may use the menu path shown in Figure 3.30.

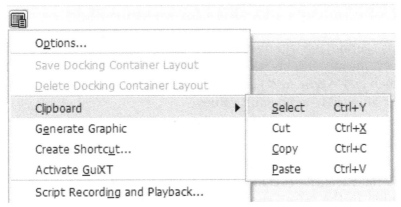

Figure 3.30: Menu Path for Copying Values

Once this is done, the cursor will change into a crosshair cursor.

- Place the cursor at the starting point of the area to be copied. Press the left mouse button to mark the top-left corner of the area to be selected. This will start the selection of the area. Keep the left mouse button pressed as you drag the cursor over the area to be copied.

NOTE: Make sure a crosshair appears for the cursor after the "CTRL+Y" keys are pressed. This means the "CTRL+Y" has been successful.

- Use the mouse to drag the cursor in order to highlight the area to be copied. Release the left mouse button to complete the selection process. A grey shaded box will appear showing the selected area.

- You may then use the "CTRL+C" keys to copy all the values that are filled in the various input fields or table lines. These may then be entered via the Paste function to any other SAP screen.

NOTE: You may use the "CTRL+Y" keys to select the content of multiple input/output fields. "CTRL+C" will then copy all the values. These may then be copied to another SAP screen or Desktop application.

3.5 Defining Default Values for an Input Field

In this section, we will discuss the default values for an Input Field. For certain input fields, there are Parameter IDs (a three-character ID, such as FWS or ABK) that are defined by SAP. In such cases, the user is allowed to set default values.

The benefit of doing this is that the user does not need to type the same value over and over again. These default values will save the user time. Whenever the user is on a screen that has the field for which the Parameter ID has been set, the default value that has been specified in the "User Data" for that input field (Parameter ID) is read and filled automatically. Another advantage of this is that one user's default value for a particular field will not affect the values of another user. A typical example of this is a currency field that may be set as a default value such as USD or GBP.

NOTE: For input fields, if applicable, values may be set as default using Parameter IDs. Parameter IDs may also be used to set user-specific settings of screens.

The procedure for defining default values for an input field is as follows:

- In order to find out whether a Parameter ID is applicable, select the input field and press "F1" in order to display the field help. The dialog will be displayed as shown in Figure 3.31.

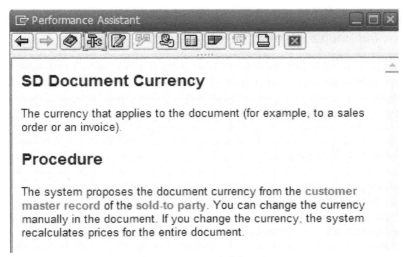

Figure 3.31: Field Help

- Then click the ▓ button. This will display the Technical Information. If the Parameter ID is applicable, a three-letter ID will be displayed as shown in Figure 3.32.

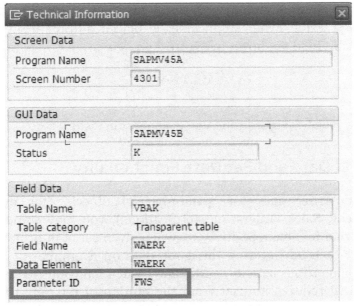

Figure 3.32: Input Help with Parameter ID

In case the Parameter ID is not defined for the field in question, the Parameter ID information will not be present.

- Once you have the Parameter ID for the field, go to the User data by following the menu path *System User Profile → Own Data*. This will lead you to the Maintain User Profile transaction. On the *Parameters* tab, enter the Parameter ID in the respective column and the default value in the *Parameter Value* column as shown in Figure 3.33.

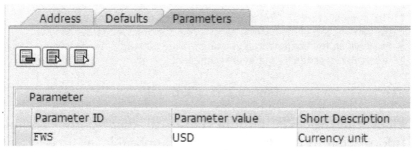

Figure 3.33: Defaults Tab

- Save your data. When you rerun the transaction, the defined default value, when applicable, is placed automatically in the relevant field as shown in Figure 3.34.

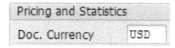

Figure 3.34: Value Appears in Field

3.6 Hold Data and Set Data Functionality

While entering data for a number of objects (for example, Employees, Sales Orders, or Notifications), you may come across screens that involve repetitive entry of a given set of information for different objects. Entering the same data on a number of screens may be a laborious activity, particularly when many entries are to be made. SAP relieves its user from the burden of retyping the same data by providing the **Hold Data/Set Data** functionality.

The Hold Data functionality allows users to save the redundant data in the SAP memory. The user types these field values for an SAP screen only once, i.e., for the first object whose information is being entered. This data then gets stored in SAP memory and is automatically made available in the respective data fields when the same screen is accessed for subsequent objects. This functionality provides a number of advantages to users:

- It lets you enter a large volume of data in SAP quickly and easily.

- For each user, SAP allocates a separate area in memory. This ensures that no clash of saved values will occur between different users.

- You may use the Hold Data/Set Data functionality for screens of all modules and sub modules.

3.6.1 Using Hold/Set Data Functionality

In order to use the Hold Data and Set Data options, follow the steps shown below:

- Call the SAP transaction on which you would like to make the redundant entries.

- As already mentioned, you only need to enter the repetitive data once. Enter these values for the first object in consideration. Do not enter a value in any field whose values are not to be copied.

- Then choose the menu option *System → User Profile → Hold Data* (see Figure 3.35).

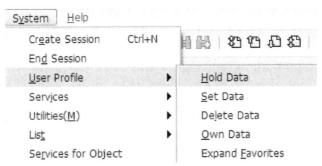

Figure 3.35: "Hold Data" Menu Path

This stores the entered data in the SAP memory. The message "Data was held" is displayed.

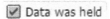

Figure 3.36 Data Was Held

The held values are displayed in red, as shown in boxes in Figure 3.37.

| Sales | Item overview | Item detail | Ordering party | Procurement | Shipping |

Req. deliv.date	D	06/05/1998	Deliver.Plant	1300	
☐ Complete dlv.			Total Weight		3.800 KG
Delivery block		▼	Volume		0.000
Billing block		▼	Pricing date	06/05/1998	
Payment terms	0002	14 Days 3%, 30/2...	Incoterms	FH	
Order reason	Marketing material f. Mailing			▼	

Figure 3.37: Held Values

You may also hold values for input fields one by one. In this case, each time you hold a value, all the held values are displayed on the input screen in red.

- When you open the same screen to enter data for subsequent objects, the saved data values are present in the relevant fields. You may also amend these values if you like.

- If you want to exclude the held value fields from data entry or navigation via the tab key, choose the menu option *System → User Profile → Set Data*. This will grey-out the field in question and will not allow editing of the field value for current and subsequent objects. Such a field will also be ignored during tab key navigation.

- When you have completed entering the data, you should delete the held values from the SAP memory. You can do this by choosing the menu option *System → User Profile → Delete Data*.

3.7 Object Manager

On the left side of the initial screen of data maintenance transactions, there may be a navigation tool known as the **Object Manager** as shown in Figure 3.38. (In this section we discuss the Object Manager as it is used in the HR transactions PA30 and PA20.)

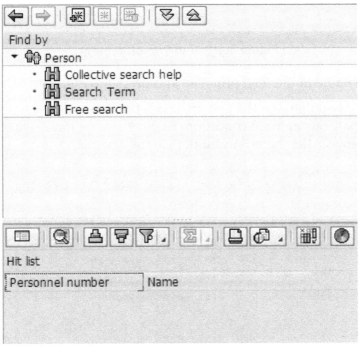

Figure 3.38 Object Manager

The search options are found on the top of the screen, and the *Hit List* area (where the values found as a result of the search are displayed) can be seen on the lower part of the screen.

There is a *Search Term* option that allows you to search in the database. In our case, we have taken the Person example, so it is the employee (or the name of the employee). Clicking the *Find by Person* option will show the dialog in Figure 3.39.

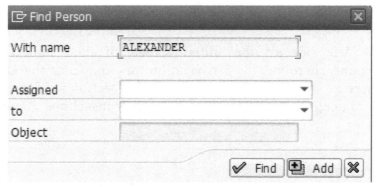

Figure 3.39: Find Person Dialog

Enter a name in the field provided and press the *Find* button.

This will populate the Hit List area with the names of the employees that satisfy our entered condition. In our case, we have searched for all employees that have "Alexander" in their name.

Hit list

Personnel number	Name
00088824	Mr. A Alexander
00088836	Mr. Ablendan Alexander
00100276	Mrs Andreas Alexander
00995563	Mrs Selma Alexander

Figure 3.40: Hit List

While you are on the Hit List, you are able to create a list of multiple names or criteria. You can do this by entering a search term and then clicking the *Enter Search Result in List* Add button. This will add the results to the existing Hit List, and then you may enter other search criteria in the *With Name* field.

Also, you may create variants that allow you to save your search criteria. To do this, click on the *Create Search Variant* 🔳 button on the toolbar. The dialog appears as shown in Figure 3.41.

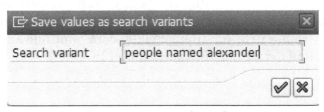

Figure 3.41: Search Variant

Enter a suitable name for your variants. Let's say we wrote "people named alexander" and then pressed the *Enter* button.

This will add a node for the newly created search variant as shown in Figure 3.42.

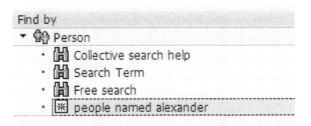

Figure 3.42: Node for Search Variant

The next time you come to the transactions, simply double-click on the relevant variants and the Hit List will be populated based on the criteria on that date. This means that, for example, when you run the saved variant "people named alexander," all of the people named Alexander will be searched for again and displayed. You may get different results each time as more people named Alexander are added to the system.

Summary of Chapter 3

This chapter discussed how to effectively enter data into the SAP system. With the information provided, you should now be able to, among other things, enter data using Data Entry Transactions, incorporate value help for Input Fields, copy multiple values from the screen, and define default values for an Input Field.

References

http://help.sap.com/saphelp_oil46csp2/helpdata/EN/85/daf1d04b
ac11d1890e0000e8322f96/content.htm

Chapter 4

Personalizing – Changing SAP Look and Feel

This chapter will cover the possible options that are available to personalize the SAP system according to your preferences. All of the settings shown in this chapter apply to one particular user; the settings of other users are not affected.

Chapter 2 described how to organize your work using Favorites. In this chapter, I will cover the specific details involved in personalizing the look and feel of the SAP system. The following topics will be covered:

- *Personalizing the initial screen,* including setting the start transaction, modifying the status fields, and changing favorites and easy access menu settings.
- *Changing SAP behavior,* including controlling cursor behavior, switching history input on or off, changing your user profile, and quick cut and paste features.
- *Changing GUI and Help settings,* including themes and fonts, adjusting dropdown list displays, personalizing message displays, and changing the display of F1 and F4 Help.

This chapter is meant to help the user create a more efficient and enjoyable SAP system. Some questions that will be answered in this chapter include:

- *How can I set the start transaction?*
- *How can I quickly cut and paste portions of text?*
- *What are my options for changing the theme and fonts?*
- *How can I personalize messages when they are displayed?*

Along the way, there will be examples and screenshots to make the task of personalizing your SAP system as easy and straightforward as possible.

4.1 Personalizing the Initial Screen

This section will discuss three changes that may be made to the default settings of the Initial SAP screen. **Personalization** can occur by setting the start transactions, modifying the status bar fields, and changing the menu and favorites display. Let us now see each of the three in detail.

4.1.1 Setting the Start Transaction

A **Start Transaction** is defined as the first transaction displayed (or that the user is taken to) after a successful logon. One of the simplest features about personalization is to set a particular transaction as the Start Transaction. You may set this to the most frequently used transaction or the first transaction that you start within your daily work.

Since this is the first screen that you are taken to, it will save time because you don't have to search within the tree or type the transaction name into the Command Field.

In order to set start transaction, from the main SAP menu choose *Extras → Set Start Transaction* as shown in Figure 4.1.

Extras	System	Help	
Display documentation			Shift+F6
Technical details			Shift+F11
Settings			Shift+F9
Set start transaction			Shift+F7

Figure 4.1: Set Start Transaction

The dialog box appears as shown in Figure 4.2.

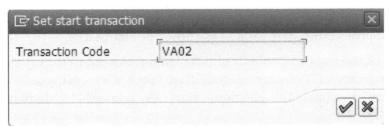

Figure 4.2: Entering Start Transaction

Enter the transaction code in the field provided and press "Enter". This will set the transaction code. The next time you log in, instead of the initial SAP easy access screen, you will be taken to the specified transaction code.

The value of the set transaction is not deleted until you change or reset it. Even if you assign value to the transaction at the end of a working day, the set transaction will remain there until your next log in (irrespective of when you log in).

4.1.2 Modifying the Status Field Display

In Chapter 1, I discussed the Status fields displayed in the Status bar. In this section, we will see how to modify the status fields display (the information given here is relevant for all SAP screens including the initial screen).

The information displayed in status bar is shown in Figure 4.3.

• System	M26 (1) 800
Client	800
User	STUDENT003
Program	SAPLSMTR_NAVIGATION
Transaction	SESSION_MANAGER
Response Time	546 ms
Interpretation Time	203 ms
Round Trips/Flushes	1/0

Figure 4.3: Status Fields

You may click on the ▼ icon to see the list of various fields that may be displayed (and their values) as shown in Figure 4.3.

Some of the options you may choose from (relevant to users) may be the Program or Transaction code that you are executing as well as your user name. In addition, you may choose to display the Response Time.

> **NOTE:** You may hide the Status fields by clicking on the ▷ icon.

To change the field displayed in the status bar, click the ▼ icon. This opens a number of options as shown in Figure 4.3.

Some of the important information that may be displayed in the status includes:

- *System and Client*: This displays the name of the system and the relevant client to which you are logged in.
- *User*: The ID with which you are logged in, for example, JONR01 etc.
- *Program:* The name of the program you are executing.
- *Transaction*: The transaction you are running.
- *Response Time*: This may simply be defined as the time it takes for the execution of a certain task (for example, a report transaction). This time is measured in milliseconds. You may execute a report to display the selection screen. Enter the data on the selection screen and click the *Execute* button. When you execute the report, it will show the time taken for the report to fetch data from the database and generate the report output.

4.1.3 Changing Favorites and Easy Access Menu Settings

For the initial SAP screen, you may change the way the Easy Access Menu and the Favorites are displayed. Let us see in detail how this is done.

To change the menu and Favorites settings, access the menu option *Extras → Settings*. This will display the dialog box as shown in Figure 4.4.

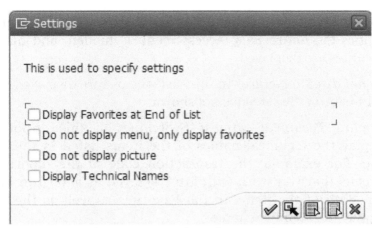

Figure 4.4: Settings for Favorites

This has four checkboxes (options), which are discussed below:

- *Display Favorites at end of list:* Choosing this option will display the Favorites at the bottom of the list in the left pane. This is shown in Figure 4.5.

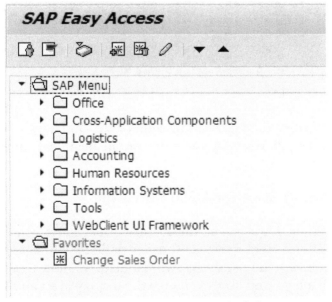

Figure 4.5: Favorites at End of List

- *Do not Display Menu, only display favorites:* If you check this option, the entire Easy Access menu is hidden, and only the Favorites are displayed.

- *Do not display picture:* In this case, the picture displayed on the right pane of the screen is not shown.

- *Display Technical names:* Switching on this option will display the technical names of the items listed in the menu tree. For example, the transaction code of the reports and screens that you work with are displayed as shown in Figure 4.6. Both of the items in the Favorites as well as the menu display the technical names.

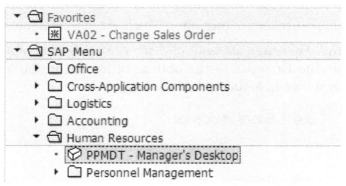

Figure 4.6: Menu Items and Favorites With Technical Names

In the figure, the transaction code of the Manager's Desktop is shown (i.e., PPMDT) by switching on the technical names.

4.2 Changing Standard GUI Settings

In this section, I will cover the features that allow you to change certain GUI and Help settings. These include how to change Theme and Fonts, how to adjust dropdown list displays, how to personalize message displays, and how to change the display of F1 and F4 Help.

> **NOTE:** The screenshots for this chapter have been taken from the latest GUI version 730. However, many of the features are also applicable to the older 710 GUI. The major difference is the way the Customizing layout options appear. In older GUI, instead of the navigation tree and nodes, there are tabs that have customization options. If you are using the older GUI, use the appropriate tab.

For most of the changes shown in this section, the Customizing Layout options are used. Click the *Customizing Local Layout* button 🖼 on the standard toolbar. From the menu that appears, choose *Options*. This will display the SAP GUI options dialog box as shown in Figure 4.7.

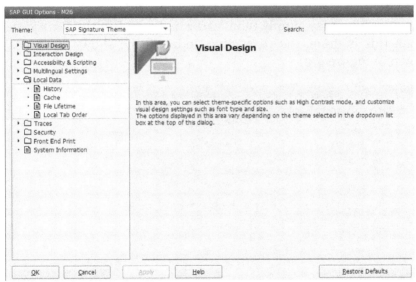

Figure 4.7: SAP GUI Customizing Options

On the left of the dialog box there is a tree that shows the different categories (or areas) that contain the various GUI customizing options. For example, we have Visual Design and Interaction Design as shown in Figure 4.8.

75

> ▸ ☐ Visual Design
> ▸ ☐ Interaction Design
> ▸ ☐ Accessibility & Scripting
> ▸ ☐ Multilingual Settings
> ▸ ☐ Local Data
> ▸ ☐ Traces
> ▸ ☐ Security
> ▸ ☐ Front End Print
> ▪ 🗎 System Information

Figure 4.8: Customizable GUI Option Areas

There is also a *Search* field that you can use to quickly look for the actual place where a particular customization option is. For example, in order to directly go to the screen for customizing error messages, you may simply type "error messages" in the *Search* field. When this is done, the respective node will be shown in italics as shown in Figure 4.9.

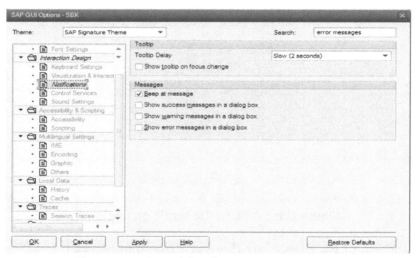

Figure 4.9: Searching for "Error Messages"

The exact node and the path for accessing it will be shown in italics, whereas the other irrelevant nodes will appear dim, making the desirable node prominent. You may double-click on this node to go directly to the customization screen (*Notifications* node in our error messages example).

> **NOTE:** If at any time you decide to restore (revert) to the default GUI settings, you may do so by using the *Restore Defaults* button (see Figure 4.9). This button will restore your default GUI settings, such as the fonts, theme, and cursor settings, back to their original form.

> **NOTE:** To access the help feature at any node or for any function, simply click the *Help* button. The necessary documentation for the screen that you are on will be displayed.

4.2.1 Changing GUI Theme and Fonts

You also have control over changing the GUI theme and the displayed fonts. In this section, we will take a closer look at how this is done.

At the top-left of the dialog box shown in Figure 4.9 is a *Theme Selection* list box. In the newer GUI version, you have the SAP "Signature Theme" selected. If you want to change the theme, choose a different theme from the dropdown list and click *Apply*.

The new theme will only be applicable when the SAP Logon pad is closed and restarted.

Within the Signature Theme you can change the default color of the SAP windows. To change the color of the Signature Theme, choose the path *Visual Design --> Color Settings*. This will be found in the left pane of the GUI Options dialog (use the Customizing Local Layout shown earlier). On the right side of the screen, select a different color (such as SAP Gold or Purple). After you have chosen a color, click the *Apply* button.

The new color will be applicable when a new SAP session is opened.

> **NOTE:** From SAP GUI 730, SAP provides a new **Corbu** Theme. This theme has a reduced contrast as compared to Signature Design and also has a different style of icons.

In addition to the theme, you have the option of changing the fonts as well as the font size displayed on the SAP screen. To do this, choose the path *Visual Design → Font settings*. The right side of the screen changes as shown in Figure 4.10 (these are the default settings).

> **NOTE:** Fixed Width Font Settings are applicable for data entered in the input fields and displayed in lists, whereas Proportional fonts are used for Captions and descriptions (for items) shown on the screen.

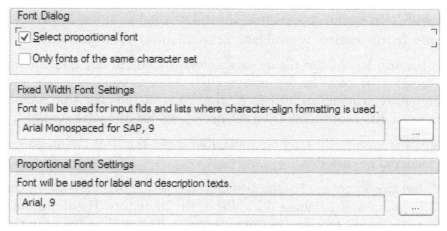

Figure 4.10: Fixed Width and Proportional Font Settings

For Fixed Width Fonts pertaining to input fields and lists, you can set the Font type as well as the size by clicking the relevant ⋯ button under the *Fixed Width Font Settings* area. This will display a *Font* selection dialog box, which can be used to specify your preferences (see figure 4.11).

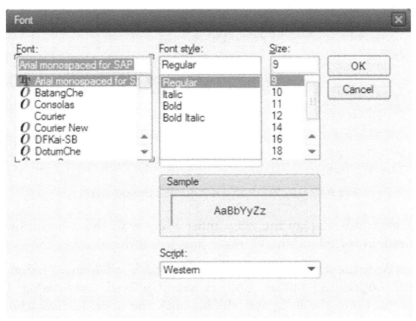

Figure 4.11: Font Selection

When you are done with your font selection, click *OK*.

If you would like to keep separate font settings for Proportional Fonts, make sure the *Select Proportional Font* checkbox at the top (under *Font dialog*) is on. Once this is done, click the ⌐...⌐ button under *Proportional Font Settings*. A similar font selection screen is displayed as shown in Figure 4.11. Here you may choose from a variety of font sizes and types according to your liking.

4.2.2 Adjusting Dropdown List Display

In addition to other features of the screen, you may modify the appearance of Dropdown lists. By default, only the description of the items is shown in the Dropdown as shown in Figure 4.12.

Address	
Address type	Permanent residence ▼
Care Of	Emergency address
Address line 1	Home address
	Home address acc. to contract
Address line 2	Hotel accomodation provided by employer
City/county	Hukou address-CN
	Mailing address
State/zip code	Nursing address
Country Key	Paycheck Location
Telephone Number	Permanent residence
	Temporary residence

Figure 4.12: Permanent Address Dropdown List

You may also display the key values along with the description, if desired, in sorted order. Let us see how this is done.

To access the Dropdown list customization, click the *Customize Local Layout* ▤ button and choose *Options*. The dialog box appears. From the left pane, double-click the node *Visualization 1* shown under *Interaction Design* (as shown in Figure 4.13).

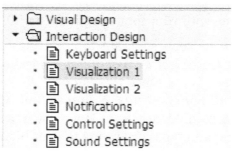

Figure 4.13: Visualization 1 node

The screen on the right appears as the one shown in Figure 4.14.

Figure 4.14: Dropdown List Customization

For older GUI versions, select the Expert tab from the dialog box that appears (Figure 4.15).

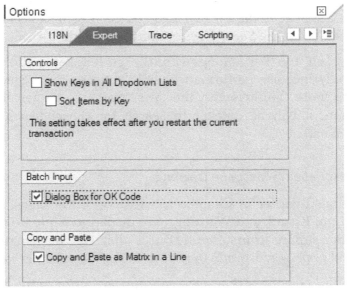

Figure 4.15: Expert tab on Older GUIs

The checkboxes displayed under the *Controls* area allow you to customize the dropdown list. By default, the two checkboxes *Show Keys in all Dropdown Lists* and *Sort Items by Key* are switched off. If the first checkbox, i.e. the one for showing keys in the list, is switched on, the keys (codes) as well as the descriptions of the items will be displayed. In this case, the dropdown lists will appear as shown in Figure 4.16.

Address		
Address type	1 Permanent residence	▼
Care Of	4	Emergency address
	3	Home address
Address line 1	7	Home address acc. to contract
Address line 2	R2	Hotel accomodation provided by employer
City/county	90	Hukou address-CN
	5	Mailing address
State/zip code	6	Nursing address
Country Key	US01	Paycheck Location
Telephone Number	1	Permanent residence
	2	Temporary residence

Figure 4.16: Address Field Options

Moreover, if you would like to sort the items by using the key, make sure that the *Sort Items By Key* checkbox is on (this checkbox will only be enabled if the *Show Keys* option is selected).

Switching on the key, along with the sorted key options, may significantly increase performance while entering data. Since most users are more familiar with the keys (codes) – rather than the description, it will be quicker to search for the code within the dropdown list.

4.2.3 Personalizing Message Displays

As mentioned earlier in Chapter 1, a variety of messages, such as Information, Errors, and Warnings, are displayed while executing a transaction. Apart from other features that can be personalized, some level of personalization may be done for messages as well.

The default behavior is that messages appear in the status bar. You may change the form of the displayed messages to more noticeable dialog boxes, which will make them appear more prominent. You may also turn a sound alert on or off when a message is displayed. One more benefit is that you can set a control for each message type, such as Information, Error, or Warning. It is possible, for example, to switch on dialog boxes display, for Warning and Errors, and let Information appear as status bar messages.

For personalizing messages, click the *Customizing Local Layout* button from the standard toolbar. From the menu, choose *Options*. From the dialog box that appears, choose the node *Notifications* under *Interaction Design* (see Figure 4.17).

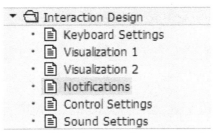

Figure 4.17: Notifications under Interaction Design

On the right side of the dialog box, a Messages area will be displayed as shown in Figure 4.18.

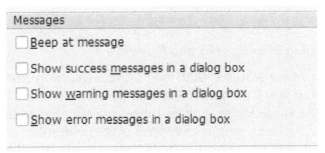

Figure 4.18: Options for Personalizing Messages

There are four checkboxes related to personalizing your messages. The *Beep at Message* checkbox allows you to have a beep sound alert occur when a message is displayed (the more important checkboxes are below this beep-related checkbox).

For each of the message types, you have a switch (checkbox) for displaying a dialog box. Check the corresponding indicator(s) for the type(s) of message that you want to see as a dialog box. If you want to see all Warnings, Errors, and Success messages as dialog boxes, check all three indicators. Figure 4.19 shows an error shown as a dialog box if the error checkbox is switched on.

Error
Enter date in the format __/__/____
OK
Help

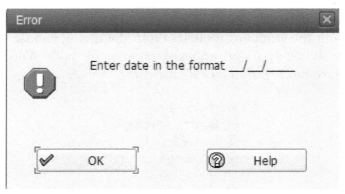

Figure 4.19: Error Message in Dialog Box

The same error previously shown in the status bar appeared as the one in Figure 4.20.

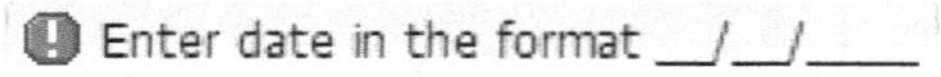

Enter date in the format __/__/____

Figure 4.20: Error Message in Status Bar

4.2.4 Changing Display of F1 and F4 Help

Apart from other features that may be changed according to your desires, some level of personalization is also possible for the F1 Input and F4 value Helps. For F1 Help, you can change the display, whereas for F4 Help, you have control over the number of values of the hit list as well as the hit list itself. Let us see in detail how this is done.

Choose the menu path *Help* → *Settings* as shown in Figure 4.21 (this is available in all SAP screens).

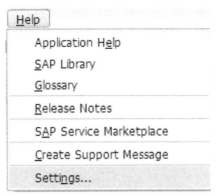

Figure 4.21: "Settings" Menu Path

The dialog box appears as shown in Figure 4.22.

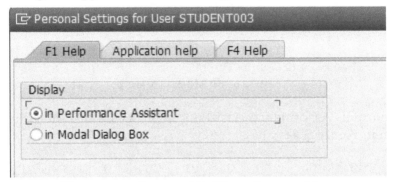

Figure 4.22: Personal Settings for your User

Two important tabs on this box are the *F1 Help* and *F4 Help*. Let us discuss them in detail.

- *F1 Help*. The previous Figure shows the F1 Help tab, which has two possible options. You may choose to display the help either in the default *Performance Assistant* display or in the form of a modal dialog box. If you choose the *Modal Dialog Box* option, the F1 help will look like the one shown in Figure 4.23.

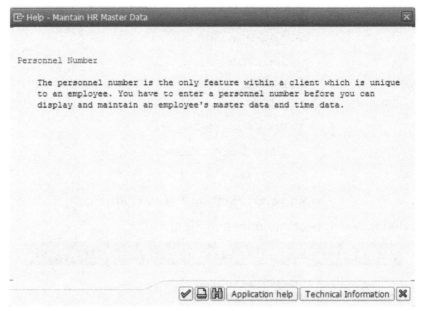

Figure 4.23: Modal F1 Help

The normal Performance Assistant help (as discussed earlier) is shown in Figure 4.24.

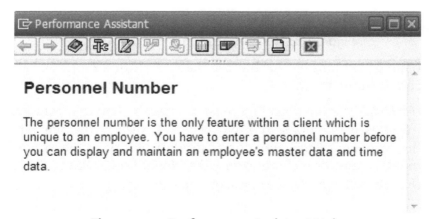

Figure 4.24: Performance Assistant Help

- *F4 Help tab.* There are some user-specific settings also related to the F4 Help. Click on the tab *F4 Help.* The appropriate screen will appear as shown in Figure 4.25.

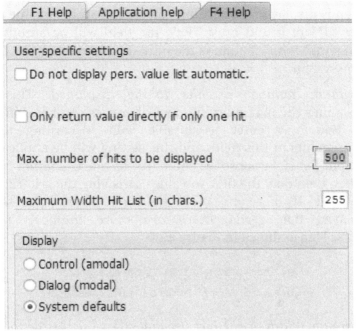

Figure 4.25: F4 Help User-specific Settings

The important checkboxes and fields of this tab are shown below:

- *Do not Display Pers. Value List Automatic.* If this checkbox is on, the Personal Value list is not displayed automatically. The main hit list is displayed. There is a *Personal List Value* button that allows you to go to your personal list. (The button is only displayed if there is at least one value in the personal list.) You may add entries into the personal list (from this screen) using the button.

If the checkbox is off, the Personal Value list is displayed. You may then go back to the main list of all possible values using the button.

- *Only Return Value directly if only one hit.* If this indicator is set, the input field is automatically filled with the value satisfying the search criteria entered, if only one value exists in the database that satisfies the given condition. In this case no hit list or value screen is displayed. For example, if we have a field name and we enter "J*" in it and press "F4", the field will be automatically filled with "John" if John is the only value starting from J stored in the system.

- *Maximum number of hits to be displayed.* This value determines the maximum number of entries displayed in the hit list. You may enter a suitable value according to your requirements in this field, and this setting will be applicable for all input fields. Suppose we enter "10" as the *Maximum Number of Hits*, then only the first 10 values satisfying the criteria will be displayed. If there are more than 10 values, a message is displayed that reads *There are more than 10 possible inputs*. This is shown in Figure 4.26.

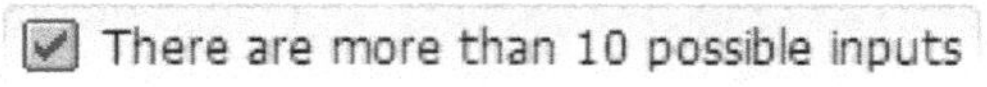

☑ There are more than 10 possible inputs

Figure 4.26: More Than 10 Inputs Message

- *Maximum Width of Hit List (in chars).* As the text denotes, this is used to control the number of columns displayed in the hit list. For example, the hit list contains three columns of 10, 15, and 30 characters of length respectively. If we want to only display the first two columns, then 25 must be entered in the *Maximum Width* field. Likewise, entering 10 will display only the first column in the list.

4.2.4.1 F4 Help: Dialog and Control Mode Radio Buttons

The Dialog and Control Modes of the F4 Help display are important. You may choose either one of them depending on your requirements. Let us take a closer look at both.

- *Dialog Mode.* When the **Dialog Mode** is selected and you press "F4" on an input field on any given SAP screen for accessing the possible list of values, the format in which the F4 list of values is displayed is shown in Figure 4.27. The values are displayed in a dialog box.

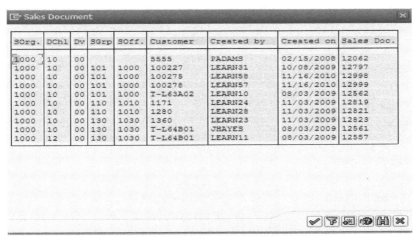

SOrg.	DChl	Dv	SGrp	SOff.	Customer	Created by	Created on	Sales Doc.
1000	10	00			5555	PADAMS	02/15/2008	12062
1000	10	00	101	1000	100227	LEARN31	10/08/2009	12797
1000	10	00	101	1000	100275	LEARN58	11/16/2010	12998
1000	10	00	101	1000	100278	LEARN57	11/16/2010	12999
1000	10	00	101	1000	T-L63A02	LEARN10	08/03/2009	12562
1000	10	00	110	1010	1171	LEARN24	11/03/2009	12819
1000	10	00	110	1010	1280	LEARN28	11/03/2009	12821
1000	10	00	130	1030	1360	LEARN23	11/03/2009	12823
1000	10	00	130	1030	T-L64B01	JHAYES	08/03/2009	12561
1000	12	00	130	1030	T-L64B01	LEARN11	08/03/2009	12557

**Figure 4.27: List of Values Generated for
F4 help of Sales Document Field**

This dialog box does not allow you to proceed with the screen on which you were working. If the list is too wide, there is a scroll bar at the bottom of the dialog box.

Before viewing the possible set of input values, if you would like the *No restrictions* checkbox to be displayed on the initial screen of your F4 help selection (i.e. on the *Restrict Value Range* screen), you need to select *Dialog Mode*. On the initial selection screen of your F4 help, the screen will appear as shown in Figure 4.28.

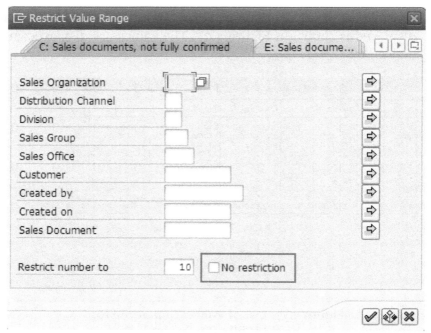

Figure 4.28: Restrict Value Range

Selecting this *No restriction* checkbox will turn off number restrictions of the list of values to be displayed. This means that if there are 10,000 values that fulfill the given criteria, all values will be displayed.

NOTE: The *No Restriction* feature is only available for F4 help list values in the Dialog Mode.

- *Control Mode.* In this case, the format that the list is displayed is shown in Figure 4.29.

Sales Document (3)	10 Entries found						
Sales document according to customer PO number				Sales documents, not fully ...			

SOrg.	DChl	Dv	SGrp	SOff.	Customer	Created by	Created on	Sales Doc.
1000	10	00			5555	PADAMS	02/15/2008	12062
1000	10	00	101	1000	100227	LEARN31	10/08/2009	12797
1000	10	00	101	1000	100275	LEARN58	11/16/2010	12998
1000	10	00	101	1000	100278	LEARN57	11/16/2010	12999
1000	10	00	101	1000	T-L63A02	LEARN10	08/03/2009	12562
1000	10	00	110	1010	1171	LEARN24	11/03/2009	12819
1000	10	00	110	1010	1280	LEARN28	11/03/2009	12821
1000	10	00	130	1030	1360	LEARN23	11/03/2009	12823
1000	10	00	130	1030	T-L64B01	JHAYES	08/03/2009	12561
1000	12	00	130	1030	T-L64B01	LEARN11	08/03/2009	12557

Figure 4.29: Search Help Control

This is the **Search Help Control** mode. It provides a variety of advantages. You may click the bar marked with _____ at the top to access the screen to further filter the values shown in the displayed list. There is also a minimize button, which will minimize the list and allow you to continue working with the SAP screen you were working on. In the case of a complex F4 search help, you may go to the other tabs while you are on the list of values.

4.3 Changing SAP Behavior

In this section, I will cover the features that allow you to change SAP behavior. These include how to control cursor behavior, how to adjust list displays on SAP screens, and how to adjust the user profile.

4.3.1 Controlling Cursor Behavior

In addition to the SAP GUI, fonts, and other visual elements, you may also change the way the cursor behaves while you work with the system. To access the cursor settings, choose the *Interaction Design* → *Keyboard Settings* node from the SAP GUI options dialog box (using the *Customizing Local Layout* button shown earlier). The screen changes as shown in Figure 4.30.

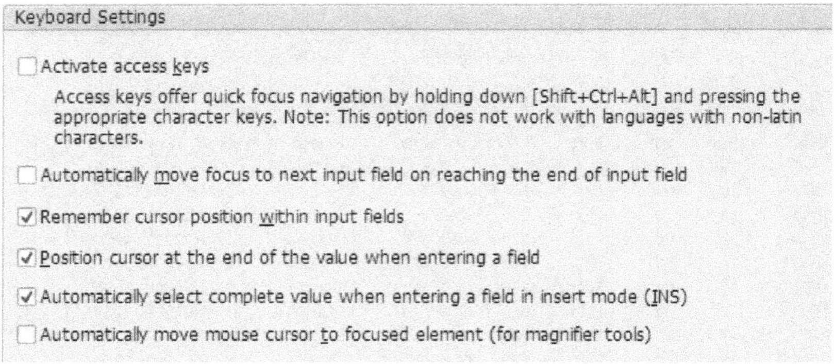

Keyboard Settings

☐ Activate access keys

Access keys offer quick focus navigation by holding down [Shift+Ctrl+Alt] and pressing the appropriate character keys. Note: This option does not work with languages with non-latin characters.

☐ Automatically move focus to next input field on reaching the end of input field

☑ Remember cursor position within input fields

☑ Position cursor at the end of the value when entering a field

☑ Automatically select complete value when entering a field in insert mode (INS)

☐ Automatically move mouse cursor to focused element (for magnifier tools)

Figure 4.30: Cursor Checkboxes on Keyboard Settings

NOTE: If you are using the earlier GUI version, access the cursor settings on the *Cursor* tab of Customizing Local Layout options.

Under *Keyboard Settings*, the following checkboxes are relevant to cursor settings. Let us discuss each in detail.

- *Automatically move focus to next input field on reaching end of field.* If this setting is on, the cursor moves automatically to the next input field (in the tab sequence) of the screen, when the first field is completely filled with data. The use of a mouse or the "Tab" key is not required. This allows you to enter data quickly without shifting the focus yourself. This is also known as **Automatic Tabbing**. By default, this checkbox is off.

- *Remember cursor position within input fields.* If this setting is on, the system remembers the position the cursor was last at within an input field. This means that if you typed partial data (some characters in an input field) and went on to enter text in another input field, the next time you focus back on the first field, the cursor will be placed after the last character (even blank spaces) that you had entered.

- *Position cursor at the end of the value when entering a field.* This checkbox, if on, brings the cursor to the end of the text entered within a field. If you enter a certain value in a field followed by spaces and then go on entering in another field, when you use the mouse to focus back on the first field, the cursor will be placed at the end of the text entered. Any blank spaces you entered will be ignored. If this setting is switched off, the cursor will be positioned to the point where the blank spaces ended.

- *Automatically select complete value when entering a field in INS mode.* When this is checked, you can overwrite the previously entered value in an input field with a single keystroke in the insert INS mode. If the focus comes to a field either with a tab or an automatic tab, the entire content of a field is selected (as shown in Figure 4.31). This makes it easy in the Insert mode to quickly change an already existing value. If you switch off this feature, the entire value will not be selected and you must delete the characters yourself.

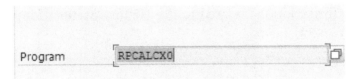

Figure 4.31: Selected Content in Field

4.3.2 Switching History Input On and Off

As mentioned earlier, SAP remembers the history of values entered in an input field. This is particularly useful when you need to input the same (or similar) value again, because you do not need to reenter the entire value. The History will help users make entries quickly and easily. Certain settings at your local layout allow you to switch the History on and off or change the way the History is displayed.

To change the History settings, access the SAP GUI options box (using the *Customize Local Layout* button as shown earlier).

Then choose the node *Local Data* → *History*. The right side of the dialog box will appear as shown in Figure 4.32.

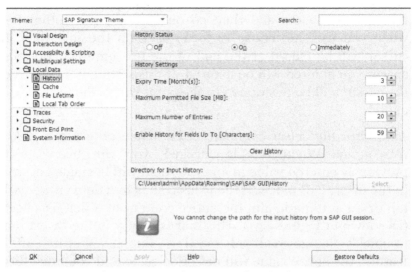

Figure 4.32: History Node Displayed

You have three options related to the History Status of input fields (see Figure 4.33).

Figure 4.33: History Status Options

The three options are discussed as follows:

- *Off*: If this option is selected, the History for all input fields will no longer be available. Additionally, the set of previously entered values will be deleted and lost, even if you switch on the History later. In some cases you will want the History for input fields to be disabled, as it may lead to confusion when making entries.

- *On*: This will switch on the History feature. The History will be displayed when you use the "Backspace" key while the cursor is on the field in question, or when you try to enter some value in the field.

- *Immediately*: In normal History On mode, the History is only displayed when the user starts entering values in the input field (or uses the "Backspace" key). Checking the *Immediately* indicator will display the History as soon as the cursor is placed on the field in question (either with a mouse click or by using the "Tab" key).

In addition to switching the History on and off, an important option is to limit the number of entries displayed in the History list. This may be done via the *History Settings* as shown in Figure 4.34.

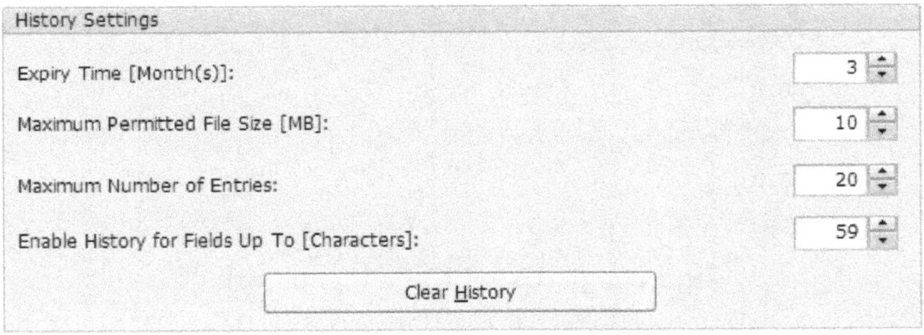

Figure 4.34: History Settings

The relevant field in this case is the *Maximum Number of Entries*. You may increase or decrease the value from the default value of 20. For example, if you type "4" in the field, the maximum entries displayed in a field's History will be 4.

If you need to clear all of the History, simply click the *Clear History* button. This will clear the History for the entire system and no history will be shown for any input field on any screen.

4.3.3 Changing Your User Profile

The Own Data within your User Profile also offers options for personalization. In this section, we will take a close look at the User Profile options available. To reach your user profile, choose the menu path *System → User Profile → Own Data* (see Figure 4.35).

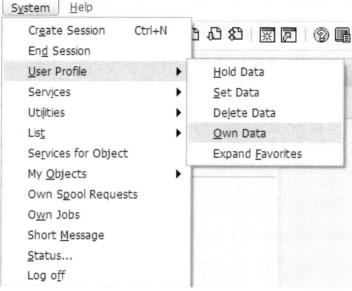

Figure 4.35: User Profile Menu Path

This will take you to the screen shown in Figure 4.36.

NOTE: In order to go directly to the *Own Data* of the User Profile, use transaction SU3.

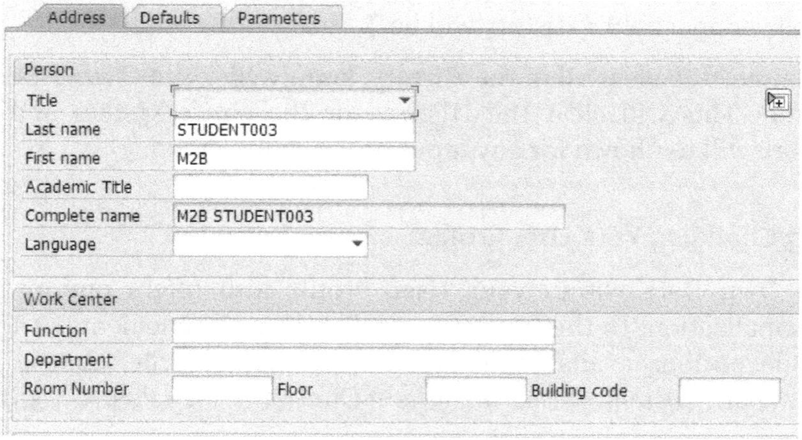

Figure 4.36: Maintain User Profile

This screen is comprised of three tabs: *Address, Defaults,* and *Parameters.* On the *Address* tab you can set the personal information related to your user ID. The various fields that may be set are Title, Last and First name, the Department, Room Number, Floor, and Building information.

The more important tab is the *Defaults* tab. Let us discuss some of the important fields on this tab that can help in personalization.

| Address | Defaults | Parameters |

Start menu	
Logon Language	
Decimal Notation	1,234,567.89 ▼
Date Format	MM/DD/YYYY ▼
Time Format (12/24h)	24 Hour Format (Example: 12:05:10) ▼

Spool Control

OutputDevice	LOCL
✓ Print immed.	
✓ Delete After Output	

Personal Time Zone

Time Zone	EST
Sys. Time Zone	CET

Figure 4.37: Defaults Tab

> **NOTE:** Once you are done with User Profile changes, save your settings. Values entered on the *Default* tab apply when you log in again. The system reads these values at the time of logon and changes itself accordingly.

- *Start Menu.* This is the area menu displayed directly after you log in to the system. It is similar to the start transaction. Use "F4" to select a value from the list that appears. If you leave this field blank, the SAP Easy Access menu will be displayed.

- *Logon Language.* This is the language applicable after you log in. All elements displayed on the user interface, such as the menu item texts, application toolbar button text, screen field labels, as well as the documentation, are in the selected logon language.

- *Decimal Notation.* The decimal notation lets you control the way the decimal figures, including amounts that are displayed on the SAP screens and lists, are formatted. The three formats in which you may display decimals are shown in Figure 4.38.

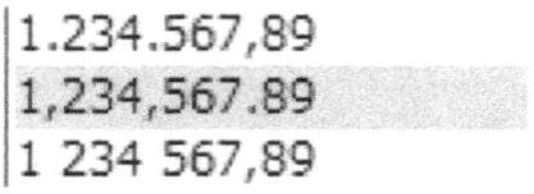

> 1.234.567,89
> 1,234,567.89
> 1 234 567,89

Figure 4.38: Decimal Formats

Choose the appropriate format based on your liking. The first format includes a period '.' for every thousand numbers and a comma will appear to denote decimals points. For example, One Million will be displayed as "1.000.000,00". In the second format, a comma will appear for every thousand and a period for the decimal. For example, in this case, One Million will appear as "1,000,000.00".

- *Date format.* Similarly, the date and time format may be set in a couple of different ways. Typical formats for the dates are MM/DD/YYYY and the DD.MM.YYYY. For example, if you choose the latter, December 31, 2014 will be displayed in screens and lists as "12/31/2014" and not "31.12.2014".

- *Spool Control.* Within the *Spool Control* area, you may set important values related to printing. In the *Output Device*, you can set your printer as the default printer to which all printing jobs will be sent.

If the *Output Immediately* checkbox is on, the print dialog box that appears while printing will also have the Output Immediately checkbox on by default. Once you select the *Print* option, the printing will be carried out immediately. You are not required to manually delete your requests from the list of Spool requests (for more on SAP printing refer to Chapter 8 - Printing Guide).

Choosing the *Delete After Output* button will delete the Spool request once your printing has been completed. If this option is not on, the requests remain in the spool list and will only be deleted by the system after a set period of time.

The *Parameters* tab within the User profile (when filled with appropriate Parameter IDs) offers some valuable personalization options. These options serve two purposes:

- If you are carrying out a task involving the repetitive entry of data in a particular field on a screen for multiple objects, you may set a default value for the input field (each time the same screen is encountered). By doing so, the default value will automatically be placed in the input field and will not require you to enter the same data into the field over and over again. This option can save a lot of time and effort when you need to enter multiple sets of repetitive data in a given field.

- Moreover, some SAP screens are programmed so that they appear or behave differently depending on the value assigned to a given Parameter ID in the profile of the user in question. For example, Parameter ID UGR (Country Grouping) may be set to denote a specific country, such as the United States or the United Kingdom. This will show the users, if applicable, the screens relevant to the country specified. (This means only that the fields specific to the country, for example the United States or the United Kingdom, will be shown.)

NOTE: A value may be defaulted by entering the field's Parameter ID in the User Profile, if the particular field has a defined ID. To check if this feature is supported for a particular field, press "F1" to access the help for the field and then choose the Technical Information button ⛭. From the box that appears, note down the Parameter ID as shown in Figure 4.39.

Figure 4.39: Reading Parameter ID

To enter a Parameter ID and assign an appropriate value, click the *Parameters* tab. A number of Parameter IDs may already be there as shown in Figure 4.40.

| Address | Defaults | Parameters |

Parameter		
Parameter ID	Parameter value	Short Description
8AP	S	FI-CA: Application in Contract Accounting
ADDRESS_SCREEN	004	Country-Spec. Addr. Layout 001 Eur., 004 USA, 005 CA, 013
BUK	1000	Company code
F4METHOD	NoActiveX	ActiveX/NoActiveX
LE_SHP_DEL_MON...	HC	Delivery Monitor: List Type
MOL	10	Personnel Country Grouping
POK	X	PD: Views (Key, Short Text, Validity, etc.)
SCL	G	Upper and lower case in source code: 'X' = lower, ' ' =upper
SOST	XXXX X X3XXX	...SOST: User Settings
WLC	X X XX X 00000	Workflow: User-specific settings

Figure 4.40: Parameter ID and Value

To enter a new Parameter ID and its value, place the cursor on a blank line. Enter the Parameter ID in the first column saying "Parameter ID". The default value must be entered in the "Parameter Value" column. Once you press "Enter", the description will automatically be filled (see Figure 4.41).

Parameter		
Parameter ID	Parameter value	Short Description
BUK	1000	Company code

Figure 4.41: Parameter ID and Value

When you are done, save your entries. The changes will then take place when you open a new session. You may change the value of the given Parameter later.

The value will only be defaulted in the given field for the user who enters the Parameter in this profile. Other users are not affected.

4.2.4 Quick Cut and Paste Feature

The **Quick Cut and Paste** is an important feature that you need to know in order to copy and paste content quickly. This feature significantly reduces the work for the user and will save plenty of time, particularly when a lot of copying and pasting of text is required.

Using this feature may change the normal SAP Copy/Cut and Paste behavior. By default this function is switched off. In order to use this function, you first need to switch on *Quick Cut and Paste*. Follow the steps shown below:

- Click the *Customize Local Layout* button 🖳 on the standard toolbar. The menu will appear as shown in Figure 4.42.

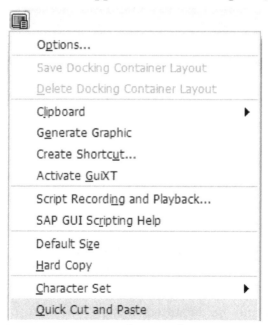

Figure 4.42 : Customize Local Layout Menu

- Click the option *Quick Cut and Paste*. This option is included in all SAP screens. Once selected, the menu option will then appear selected to indicate that the Quick Cut and Paste function has been switched on (see Figure 4.43).

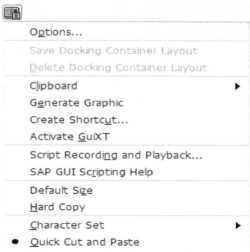

Figure 4.43: Quick Cut and Paste

- This function enables you to copy text simply by selecting it. Within the SAP screens, you may then copy texts from either the input or output fields by selecting it via the mouse left-click. Once the text is copied, it may be pasted in other places within SAP or in other desktop applications.

- For pasting, simply right-click while placing the cursor on the field in which the copied text is to be placed. This will automatically copy the text into the field.

> **NOTE:** Switching on "Quick Cut and Paste" will allow you to copy text simply by selecting it from any SAP screen. (No copying is required either with "CTRL+C" keys or mouse right-click.) Likewise, you can Paste text simply with a mouse right-click.

Summary of Chapter 4

This chapter discussed changes that can be made to personalize the look and feel of your SAP system. With these directions, you should now be able to personalize your initial screen, change various SAP behaviors, and also change the GUI and Help settings. Utilizing these techniques in your SAP system will make for a more efficient and pleasant working experience.

Chapter 5

Executing Report Transactions and Downloading Output

In this chapter, we will discuss the various ways in which you may execute report transactions and download their output.

This chapter will cover the following important topics:

- *Types of Report Outputs*
- *Online Execution of Reports*
- *Executing Reports in Background*
- *Downloading List Output*
- *Desktop Shortcuts for Programs/Reports*

This chapter will begin with the procedures that are available for executing and generating output. It will then move into discussing how to save the outputs on your local PC in various formats. The chapter will end with a discussion on various desktop shortcuts that you may use for both programs and reports.

Some questions to be answered in this chapter include:

- *How can I execute a report?*
- *What are the different formats that can be used for displaying reports?*
- *How do I execute reports in Background Mode?*
- *How can I download a list onto my PC?*

Throughout the chapter, there will be examples and screenshots to help the reader understand the process of executing reports and saving outputs to their PC. In this chapter the terms Report, Report Program, and Report Transaction will be used interchangeably.

5.1 Types of Report Outputs

In this section, we will see some of the various formats in which data is outputted by Report programs. These are ABAP List Viewer (ALV), classic ABAP List, Smart forms, and Adobe PDF Forms. Let us review them one by one.

5.1.1 ABAP List Output and ALV format

One format that may be used for displaying reports is the **ABAP List** format. You may get the report output in a typical list format as shown in Figure 5.1.

```
Table:           SCARR
Displayed Fields:  4 of   5       Fixed Columns:
```

Client	Airline	Airline	Airline Currency
800	AA	American Airlines	USD
800	AB	Air Berlin	EUR
800	AC	Air Canada	CAD
800	AF	Air France	EUR
800	AZ	Alitalia	EUR
800	BA	British Airways	GBP
800	CO	Continental Airlines	USD
800	DL	Delta Airlines	USD
800	FJ	Air Pacific	USD
800	JL	Japan Airlines	JPY
800	LH	Lufthansa	EUR
800	NG	Lauda Air	EUR
800	NW	Northwest Airlines	USD
800	QF	Qantas Airways	AUD
800	SA	South African Air.	ZAR
800	SQ	Singapore Airlines	SGD
800	SR	Swiss	CHF
800	UA	United Airlines	USD

Figure 5.1: Report Output in List Format

Lines separate the displayed columns, and the text may be represented by different colors.

In addition to the ABAP list, a popular format that users come across while running SAP report programs is the ALV format (or more precisely, **SAP List Viewer**). The ALV output has a number of functions on the toolbar that you may perform on the displayed data. A typical ALV output is shown in Figure 5.2.

> **NOTE:** For detailed information on ALV outputs and the functions supported, please refer to the Chapter 7 - ALV Displays.

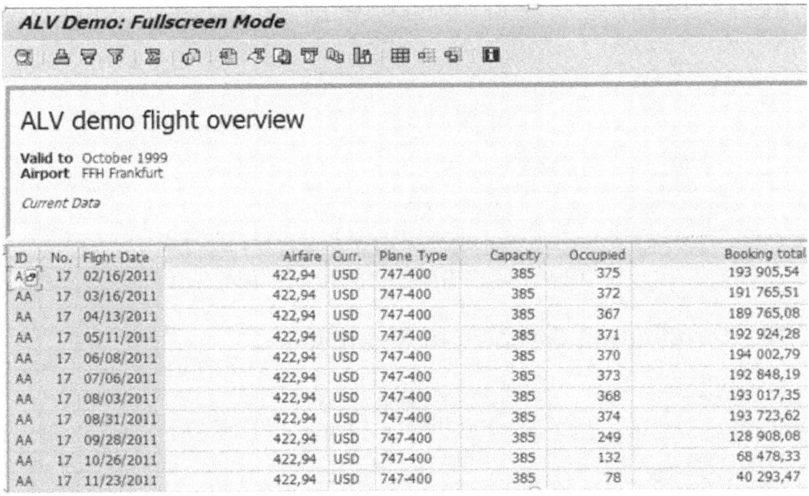

ID	No.	Flight Date	Airfare	Curr.	Plane Type	Capacity	Occupied	Booking total
AA	17	02/16/2011	422,94	USD	747-400	385	375	193 905,54
AA	17	03/16/2011	422,94	USD	747-400	385	372	191 765,51
AA	17	04/13/2011	422,94	USD	747-400	385	367	189 765,08
AA	17	05/11/2011	422,94	USD	747-400	385	371	192 924,28
AA	17	06/08/2011	422,94	USD	747-400	385	370	194 002,79
AA	17	07/06/2011	422,94	USD	747-400	385	373	192 848,19
AA	17	08/03/2011	422,94	USD	747-400	385	368	193 017,35
AA	17	08/31/2011	422,94	USD	747-400	385	374	193 723,62
AA	17	09/28/2011	422,94	USD	747-400	385	249	128 908,08
AA	17	10/26/2011	422,94	USD	747-400	385	132	68 478,33
AA	17	11/23/2011	422,94	USD	747-400	385	78	40 293,47

Figure 5.2: ALV Output

5.1.2 Form Output

Apart from the list and ALV output, you may also run programs and they may generate a form-like output. There are typically two possible formats: **Smart Form** and **Adobe Forms** in PDF format. A print preview is shown for the two types of forms in the screen.

The Smart form output is shown in Figure 5.3.

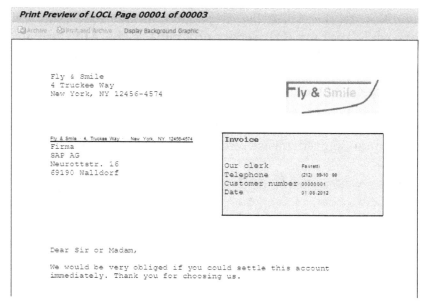

Figure 5.3: Smart Form Output

The PDF form output is shown in Figure 5.4.

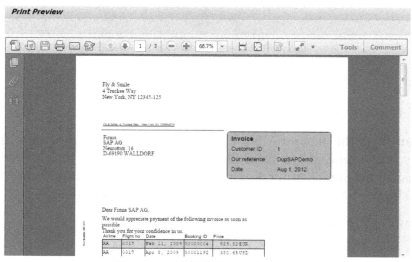

Figure 5.4: PDF Form Output

You may print the forms or view a Print Preview. The form opens in a PDF Viewer within the SAP window, and all PDF functions such as "*Save a Copy*," "*Zoom in*", and "*Zoom out*" are available on the user screen. In addition to the read-only mode, forms may be editable (Interactive) depending on the requirement.

5.2 Online Execution of Reports

As mentioned earlier, a report transaction may be executed from the SAP Easy Access Menu by double-clicking the relevant node in the SAP Easy Access Menu. Alternately, you may choose the transaction node from Favorites and then double-click (as shown in Chapter 2) or choose menu option *Edit → Execute*.

For online execution of a report transaction, you may also type the transaction code in the Command field and press "Enter". All of the above options will take you to the selection screen of the report program. A typical selection screen is shown in Figure 5.5.

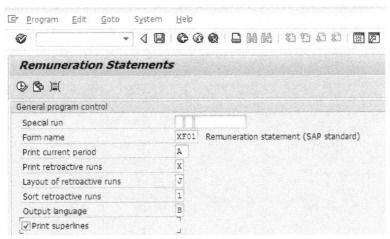

Figure 5.5: Selection Screen

You may then enter the appropriate entries on the screen and press "F8" to generate the output.

For more information on how to fill the selection screen, refer to Chapter 6 - Mastering Selection Screens.

Apart from the online execution, you may also run program reports in background. This is useful for long-running reports. The output of the report is sent to the spool and may be printed later by the user.

5.3 Executing Reports in Background

For long-running report programs, you may execute them in **Background mode**. For running the report in background, first run the transaction so that the report selection screen appears. Then, choose the option *Execute in Background*. Alternately, you may press the "F9" key. The print dialog appears as shown in Figure 5.6.

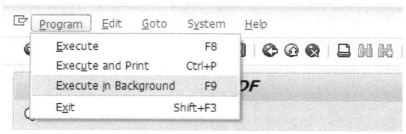

Figure 5.6: Execute in Background

Then you will see the scheduler dialog box as shown in Figure 5.7.

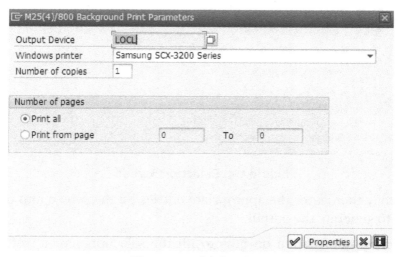

Figure 5.7: Dialog Box

Once done, the dialog box appears for specifying the Start Time.

Test Program: Generate PDF

M25(4)/800 Start Time

| Immediate | Date/Time | After job | After event | At operation mode | >.. |

Date/Time

After job   At operation mode

After event

✓ Check 🖫 ✖

Figure 5.8: Start Time Dialog Box

This is an important dialog box, as we need to specify the exact time at which you want the Report to start and then stop. For example, we can specify either Immediate or any specific Date and Time when the program execution should start.

Click the *Date/Time* button. This will show the fields required to specify the date and time for the report in question.

Date/Time

| Scheduled start | Date | 01/01/2012 | Time | 20:12:55 |
| No Start After | Date | | Time | |

Figure 5.9: Date/Time

Enter suitable values in the Scheduled Start date and time fields as shown in Figure 5.9.

The Periodic job indicator may be checked if you would like to run the job periodically as shown in Figure 5.10.

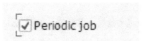

Figure 5.10: Periodic Job

When the indicator is checked, it will display the dialog box as shown in Figure 5.11

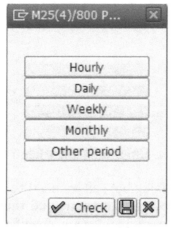

Figure 5.11: Periodic Job Dialog Box

Check the relevant button for your requirement, such as hourly, daily, or weekly. Finally, click the *Check* button in order to ensure the correctness of your entered data.

Once you have made all relevant settings, make sure to click the *Save* button on the Start Time dialog box shown in Figure 5.8. The report will then be scheduled for background execution instead of online (foreground) execution. The output is then sent to a spool request.

5.4 Downloading List Output

A typical ABAP list was shown earlier in Figure 5.1. Let's suppose that we need to download it on our PC. In this section, we will see in detail the process of saving report outputs on your local PC in various formats.

You are able to download outputs in a number of formats, such as simple text format, rich text format (RTF), Excel, or HTML formats. While you are on the list output, you may save the list output on your local PC by following the menu path *List* → *Save/Send* → *File*.

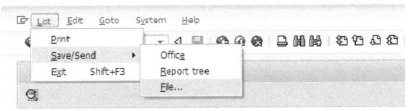

Figure 5.12: Saving List Output

The dialog box appears as shown in Figure 5.13.

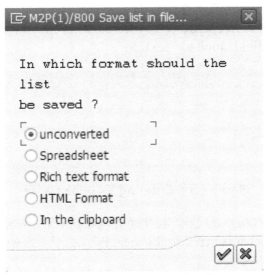

Figure 5.13: Save List in File

Choose the appropriate option in which you want the output to be downloaded. There are a number of possible formats.

The unconverted format lets you store the output in a simple text file. Choosing this option will display the dialog shown in Figure 5.14.

> **NOTE:** For downloading ALV in Excel etc. refer to the chapter ALV Outputs.

Figure 5.14: Storing Output in Text File

You may then enter a suitable file name and choose a suitable directory, for example, the Desktop. By default, the SAP work directory appears in the Directory field. Enter a suitable file name in the *File Name* field, such as "text.txt".

Figure 5.15: Entering TXT File Name

Next, click the *Generate* button. The message will appear showing the number of bytes transferred to the local PC, i.e., the size of the file.

Figure 5.16: Number of Bytes Transferred

The text file is a simple unformatted file.

Moreover, your ABAP list with its various columns may also be downloaded in the Excel format. In this case, choose the Spreadsheet option shown in Figure 5.13.

This will display a dialog box shown earlier. Enter a suitable name in the field as shown in Figure 5.17.

Figure 5.17: Saving as Excel File

An Excel file is created on the Desktop and may be viewed later.

You can also download the ABAP list output in HTML format. Or you may choose the Rich Text format (RTF) by choosing the relevant options shown.

If a file by that name already exists, then choose the *Replace* button in order to replace the file with your new data.

5.5 Desktop Shortcuts for Programs/Reports

For quick execution of frequently used programs, SAP also allows you to create shortcuts on the desktop of your PC. This functionality provides many advantages to users:

- Instead of searching for programs or remembering transaction codes, the users may simply double-click the shortcut on the desktop. This saves users' time by letting them quickly execute their most used transactions or programs.
- You may create as many shortcuts as you like.
- The shortcut only allows authorized users to execute the program or transaction in question. If no connection to SAP exists, the system first verifies the user name and password before allowing access to the transaction.

To create shortcuts, follow the steps shown below:

- Select an item from the SAP Easy Access Menu (or from the Favorites) and right-click to access the context menu as shown in Figure 5.18.

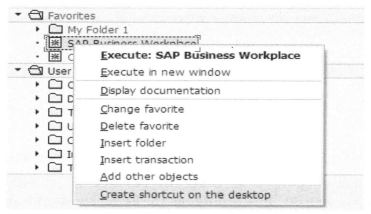

Figure 5.18: Context menu of a Menu Node

- Choose the option *Create shortcut on the desktop*. A message *Shortcut created on the desktop* is displayed.

Shortcut created on the desktop

Figure 5.19: Message of Shortcut Creation

A shortcut then appears on the desktop with an SAP icon as shown in Figure 5.20.

Figure 5.20: Desktop Shortcut

To execute the given program or transaction, simply double-click on the shortcut. The relevant transaction screen will appear if you are already logged into the system. In case you are not, you are asked to enter your user ID and password before going to the transaction.

Summary of Chapter 5

This chapter outlined how to execute reports and save outputs on your PC. With the information provided, you should now be able to identify the different formats that can be used to display reports, execute reports in Background Mode, save lists and other outputs to your PC, and use desktop shortcuts for programs and reports.

Chapter 6

Mastering Selection Screens

This chapter will focus on selection screens and the various ways that you can make them more efficient and useful. I will discuss, in detail, the important concepts related to typical report selection screens within the SAP arena. The following topics will be covered:

- *Components of Selection Screens*, including checkboxes, radio buttons, and single value input fields.

- *Selection Criteria (Options) or Ranges*, including how to specify multiple single values and ranges and how to enter mass data on a program screen.

- *Selection Screen Variants*, including how to retrieve, create, change, and delete Variants.

This chapter will enable the reader to master the various elements of a typical selection screen and will ensure a more user friendly and efficient working experience. It will answer such questions as:

- *How can I define my selection criteria?*

- *How can I copy values from the clipboard and paste them into the SAP selection screen?*

- *What are the advantages of Variants?*

There will be examples and screen shots to guide you in the process of mastering the various concepts within the selection screens.

6.1 Selection Screen Components: An Overview

In this section, I will cover the details of a typical report **Selection Screen** (and screen elements) that you may encounter within the SAP arena.

A typical selection screen for programs is shown in Figure 6.1.

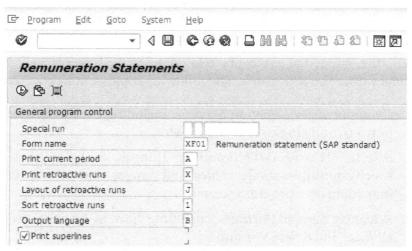

Figure 6.1: Selection Screen

There may be a number of blocks within a selection screen. Each block is comprised of input fields that can allow either single value input fields or ranges known as **Selection Options**. In addition, you may have radio buttons and checkboxes on the screen.

> **NOTE:** On a selection screen, you may have input fields that are mandatory, meaning the program will not execute until the field(s) is (are) filled with appropriate data. The required field appears with a tick mark in it as shown in Figure 6.2.

Figure 6.2: Mandatory Input field

You enter the data on the screen and then choose the *Execute* button. Alternately, you may press "F8" to execute the report based on your selection criteria. In case you need to enter data in a required (mandatory) single input or range field, an error is issued as shown in Figure 6.3.

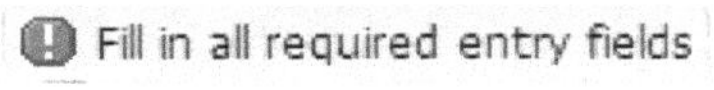

Fill in all required entry fields

Figure 6.3: Error

6.1.1 Checkbox

A typical checkbox is shown in Figure 6.4.

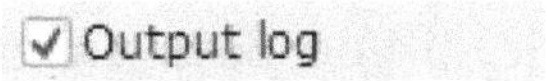

☑ Output log

Figure 6.4: Checkbox

For example, you may have an *Output Log* checkbox. This may, by default, be On or Off. The program executes and displays results based on the checkbox condition specified. For example, if you have an *Output Log* checkbox as shown in Figure 6.4, it will display the Log only if the checkbox is selected. A screen can contain a number of checkboxes, and these are all independent of each other. You may check all of the checkboxes or choose to leave them all unchecked.

Within the screen, you may also have a *Test run* checkbox. These are typical of programs that update the database. If you have Test run on, all the results will be generated (in simulation mode) and calculated, but it will not be posted to the database.

6.1.2 Radio Buttons

There are a number of choices available in the case of a radio button. By default, upon the execution of the report, one of the choices will be checked. You may then decide which of the other choices to select. The radio buttons are in groups, and only one radio button choice within a group may be selected. A screen may contain a number of radio button groups.

6.1.3 Single Value Input Fields

Single Value or Parameters are single input fields that do not allow you to specify range (as shown in Figure 6.5).

Figure 6.5: A Single Value Input Field

A single field may take numbers, texts, and dates as input. If a single input field is left blank, only the data pertaining to the blank value of that field will be displayed.

Based on a radio button selection or a checkbox, it is possible that input fields may become visible or invisible, or they may be enabled or disabled. For example, if you have an input field linked to the radio button option *Layout for Remun Statement*, it may be possible that the given field is only enabled when the relevant radio button option is selected.

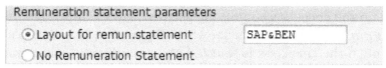

Figure 6.6: Radio Button Option

You may have an F4 search help associated with a single input field for possible values. For example, in the case of a date, you may use "F4" to choose an appropriate date.

Note: At any time, you may access the F1 help/information for an input field.

6.2 Selection Criteria (Options) or Ranges

One of the most important elements that may exist within a selection screen is the Selection option or criteria — also termed as Ranges. This allows you to enter a range of values that are to be read from the database. If used wisely, it can greatly reduce the work of the user as well as the load on the system. It can also improve the system's performance.

> **NOTE:** For selection criteria, F1 and F4 helps are also available.

A typical selection option is shown in Figure 6.7.

Figure 6.7: Selection Criteria

There are two input fields on the selection screen (a *Low* and *High* field) as well as an Extension (arrow button) on the right.

There are many options available to you in order to define your criteria. These options include entering single values, one range, or multiple ranges within the input fields. You may also keep the field blank by not entering any data. If the field is left blank, all entries will be fetched from the database. For example, if you enter a report on the personnel number 000001, the report will only show the data of that employee. Keeping the personnel number blank will display all employees.

In its simplest form, the selection criteria allow you to enter a range as well as single values. For example, if you enter the date range 01.01.2011 and 31.12.2011, the system will show all records falling between 1 January 2011 and 31 December 2011. On the other hand, if we enter 01.01.2011 in the first input field and leave the second input field blank, only records that are valid at 01.01.2011 will be shown. If the two input fields are left blank, all data will be shown regardless of what dates they belong to.

6.2.1 Specifying a Single Value or Range

The ranges may accept input in the form of numbers or dates as well as character fields such as names.

The selection criteria (or ranges) have a number of selection options attached for each input field. To display the various selection options and signs applicable, keep the cursor on the input field and double-click. The various selection options appear.

Depending on the type of input field as well as the value entered before the double-click, ten selection options may appear. These selection options are listed in Figure 6.8 along with their meanings.

Selection Option	Meaning
≠	Not Equal To
<	Less Than
>	Greater Than
≤	Less Than or Equal To
≥	Greater than or equal to
=	Equal To
[*]	Pattern
[*[	Exclude Pattern
[ ]	Range
][	Outside Range

Figure 6.8: Selection Options

The above options are used with two available signs, namely *Include* and *Exclude*. On the selection options dialog, you may use the ☐ Select button to switch on the Include sign, whereas the ⦿ Exclude from Selection button is used for specifying the Exclude sign. When the Exclude sign is on, the various selection options will appear red in color.

Here are some examples that will help clarify the usage and explore the power of selection criteria.

• *Specifying Number Ranges*: Suppose you have a range for employee numbers that you need to enter and you want to specify them on an interval of numbers between 1 and 100. To do this, simply enter "1" in the lower field and "100" in the upper field as shown in Figure 6.9.

Figure 6.9: Selecting Numbers 1 to 100

On the other hand, there are a number of options available to deselect employees from 1 to 100. This means include all employee numbers except for those falling within the range of 1 to 100. One option for this is to use the *Outside Range* selection option. To do this, enter the values "1" and "100" in the lower and upper fields respectively, and then double-click the lower range field. The screen appears as shown in Figure 6.10.

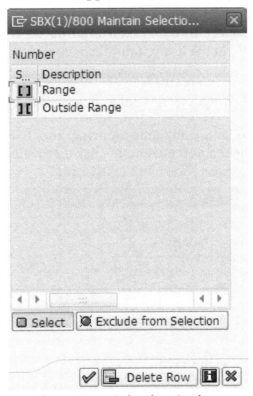

Figure 6.10: Selection Options

Choose the option *Outside Range* and press "Enter". The field will then appear as shown in Figure 6.11.

Figure 6.11: Selecting All Outside Range

This will exclude employees from 1 to 100 from the selection.

Alternately, from the pop-up shown in Figure 6.10, you may press the *Exclude from Selection* option, choose the *Range* option, and press "Enter". The field will then appear as shown in Figure 6.12.

Figure 6.12: Exclude all numbers from 1 to 100

- *Specifying Patterns.* In case you have a name range field and you want to select all names starting from P, you can do so by specifying "P*" in the lower input field, as shown in Figure 6.13.

Figure 6.13: "P*" entered in Input field

If you need to ignore all names starting from P, enter "P*" in the lower input field and then double-click on the field to display the selection options as shown in Figure 6.14.

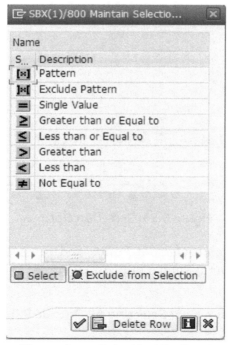

Figure 6.14: Selection Options

Select the *Exclude Pattern* option and press "Enter". The input field will then look like the one shown in Figure 6.15.

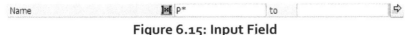

Figure 6.15: Input Field

Another way to eliminate all names starting with P is to click the *Exclude from Selection* button and then choose the option *Pattern*. The input field should look like the one shown in Figure 6.16.

Figure 6.16: Eliminating "P"

In the above-mentioned ways, you may exclude all names starting from P.

- *Ignoring Blank Spaces*. To ignore all blank spaces, double-click on the lower input field. The options appear as shown in Figure 6.17.

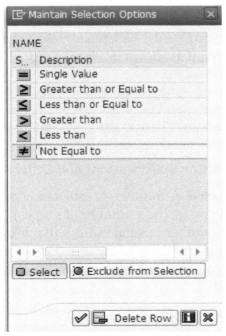

Figure 6.17: "Not Equal to" Option

Select the ≠ (*Not Equal to*) option, and click the *Save* button. The input field will then look like the one shown in Figure 6.18.

Figure 6.18: Input Field

This ensures that blank values are not used in the selection criteria.

- *Specifying Date Selection.* Suppose you have a date field range and you need to specify all dates but ignore the date 01 December 2012. You must select the *Not Equal to* option and specify the date 12/01/2012 in the lower input field, as shown in Figure 6.19.

Figure 6.19: "Not Equal To" Option

Likewise, if we need to specify that all dates greater than or equal to 01/01/2013 must be fetched, select the ≥ (*Greater than or Equal to)* option as shown in Figure 6.20.

Figure 6.20: "Greater than" Option for Dates

6.2.2 Multiple Selection Specifications and Other Available Options

Selection options have a number of other advanced options. You may enter a simple range (or a number of ranges), or you may enter a single value or a number of single values that are to be selected. In addition, you may specify any range of values or single values that are to be excluded from the selected or displayed data. Let us discuss them in detail.

Selection options allow you to:

- Enter one or more single values that need to be in the selection criteria.

- Enter one or more range values that are to be included in the selection.

- Specify one or more single values that are to be excluded from the selection.

- Specify a range of values that are to be excluded from the selection.

To enter multiple single values and/or ranges, click the ⇨ button next to the selection criteria. The screen appears as shown in Figure 6.21.

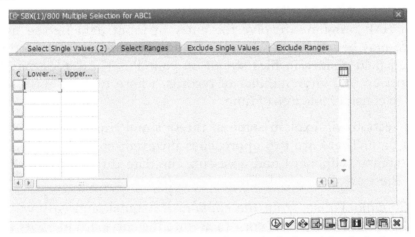

Figure 6.21: Values/Ranges to be Included and Excluded

6.2.2.1 Specifying Multiple Single Values and Ranges

Within the dialog box (shown in Figure 6.21), you may enter a number of single values and ranges that you would like to include or exclude in your selection. There are four tabs, namely, *Select Single Values, Select Ranges, Exclude Single Values,* and *Exclude Ranges.*

Suppose you have a number field and you need to see the data for all numbers ranging from 1 to 1000 and from 3000 to 4000, and also the two numbers 2005 and 2008. However, you want the numbers ranging from 50 to 65 to be omitted from the selection. In this case, three tabs in the *Multiple Selection* screen must be filled in as follows: The range "1"- "1000" and "3000" – "4000" will be entered on the *Ranges* tab.

On the *Single* tab, you will enter the two numbers "2005" and "2008". To omit the numbers from 50 to 65, you should enter the range "50" – "65" on the *Exclude* tab.

6.2.2.2 Entering Mass Data on Program Screen

Apart from the entry functions, a number of other important functions are supported on the Multiple Selection screen. Let us discuss them one by one.

Most SAP programs involve the entry of input data by the user. There may be situations when the data to be entered into a certain screen field resides in files stored on your PC. These files may be comprised of a large number of records, whose manual entry may lead to considerable loss of time.

This section will explain some of the tips and tricks used to enter such data. There are two approaches involved: copying data using the memory clipboard and accessing the data directly from a text file. These are discussed below:

- *Copying Values from the clipboard.* A quick and easy way to enter values is to first copy them into the clipboard memory and then paste them into the SAP selection screen.

  From Microsoft Word or Excel, select the column of values that are to be entered using the "CTRL+C" keys. You may also copy data from other SAP screens or lists using the "CTRL+Y" and "CTRL+C" keys.

  Click the ⇨ button next to the field in which the file values are to be entered. This will display the *Multiple Selection* screen as shown in Figure 6.22.

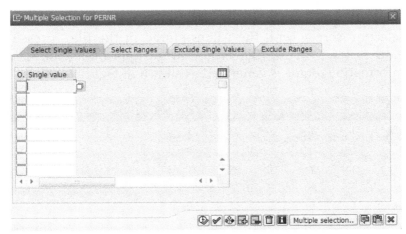

Figure 6.22: Multiple Selection Screen for Field Personnel Number

On this screen, click the ⬚ button. The values stored in the clipboard are pasted into the *Single Values* column of the screen field.

- *Copying Values directly from a Text File.* You may also copy values directly from a text file stored on the hard drive of your PC.

  On the *Multiple Selection* screen, click the ⬚ button. A dialog box appears as shown in Figure 6.23.

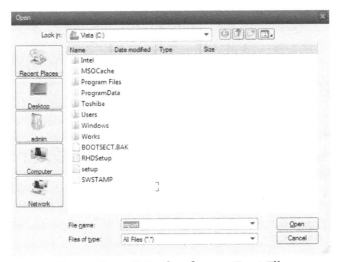

Figure 6.23: Entering from a Text File

131

Select the file and click the *Open* button. This populates the selection screen with the values stored in the file. In case the data residing in the file is not in an appropriate format, an information dialog is generated as shown in Figure 6.24.

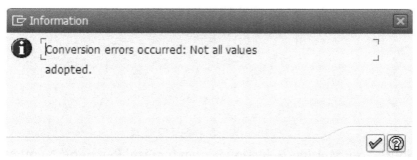

Figure 6.24: Conversion Error Dialog

6.3 Selection Screen Variants

Variants are simply defined as the (stored) set of input values for a given field. In a case where you need to run a report involving a large number of input fields that you do not want to memorize, you may choose to read from the stored set of input values provided by the Variant. This is beneficial in that it will relieve the user from the burden of entering the values over again.

> **NOTE:** Variants store all inputs specified on the selection screen, including radio button options, checkboxes, and the single and range input fields.

Variants provide the following advantages:

- Saves time by storing the values that are to be entered for a given set of fields on the user screen.

- Instead of hard-coded values assigned to fields, you may also have the option of setting dynamic values, such as the value of system date, etc.

- You may also make fields mandatory or invisible depending on user settings.

- Variants also store the signs and selection options of any range of input fields.

The user may change the values retrieved from the selected Variant, and a number of Variants may be defined for a particular report. You may name them according to the area for which they are applicable or for the frequency with which they are run. For example, you may name a Variant "Monthly" and "Yearly" to denote the yearly or monthly execution of a report.

In the next sections we will take a close look at how Variants are defined and retrieved.

6.3.1 Retrieving Variants

To access a given Variant, proceed as follows:

- From the program selection screen, choose the menu option *Variants → Get Variants*. Alternately, you may choose the keys "Shift+F5" shortcut or click on the ⏏ button on the application toolbar (the button appears if at least one variant exists). The dialog appears as shown in Figure 6.25.

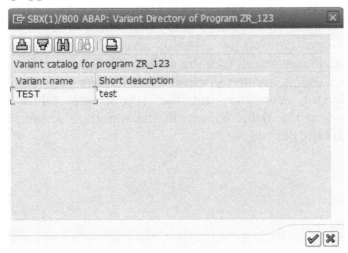

Figure 6.25: Variant Directory

You may then choose from the list the Variant that you would like to retrieve. In case you have a number of Variants defined by a number of users, a dialog box appears in which you can enter your user ID in the *Created By* field and then choose the 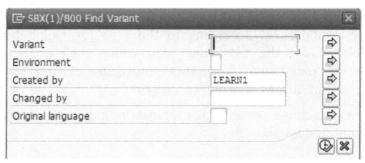 button to display the Variants defined by you (see Figure 6.26).

Figure 6.26: Find Variant

You may then choose the Variant you are interested in.

6.3.2 Creating Variants

Tor create Variants, go to the selection screen of the program, enter the values in the appropriate fields that you wish to save in Variant form, and click the *Save* button. This leads you to the *Variant Attributes* screen as shown in Figure 6.27.

For each input field on the selection screen, a row appears on the Variant attributes screen (see the *Objects for Selection Screen* table in Figure 6.27). A number of checkboxes appear for controlling the field behavior. You may set the appropriate values for the checkboxes of the fields shown on the report selection screen in order to get the desired result.

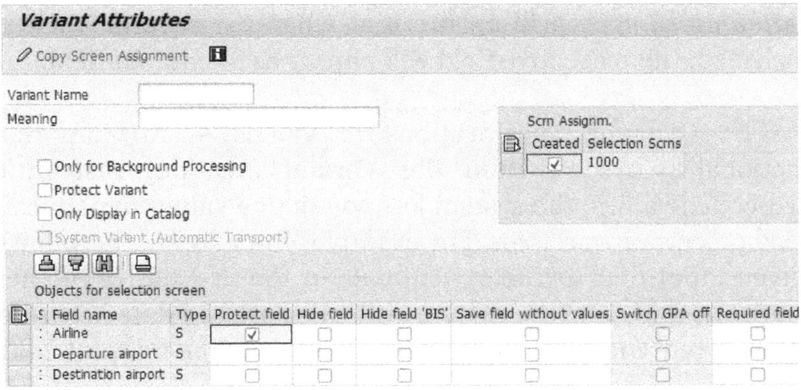

Figure 6.27: Variant Attributes

Enter a Variant name and meaning in the fields provided. If you do not want the Variant to appear when the program is executed in Online/dialog mode, check the indicator *Only for Background Processing*. If you do not want the Variant to be changed by any users, make sure the *Protect Variant* checkbox is selected. Then you need to fill the Objects table, the most important fields of which are shown below:

- *Field Name.* This is the long text of the input field that appears on the selection screen.

- *Protect Field.* If the Protect Field indicator is checked for a particular field, input is not allowed for the given field. All input fields that have this checkbox selected appear as grey fields when the relevant Variant is used.

- *Hide Field.* This may be used to hide or make fields invisible that are not meant for display. Your screen may consist of a number of unwanted fields, and you may hide them as you wish.

- *Save Field Without Values.* In case you want to ignore a particular field or fields during Variant selection and retrieval, you can save Variants without any values for the fields by clicking this indicator. For example, if you have a *Date* field on the screen and you check the *Save Field without Values* indicator, upon retrieval of the Variant, the value entered in the Date field on the screen is not affected.

135

- *Mandatory*. This will ensure that when the current Variant is selected, the respective field will appear as a required field.

> **NOTE:** Dynamic Specifications of Values — An important functionality exists within the Variant creation. Instead of hard-coded values, the system lets you define values dynamically based on certain variables. For example, you may set the value of a given input field as the system date or the first day of the next month. In this case, the system will calculate the date according to the current month and year and display it in the relevant field.

Let us see how we can specify in the Variant that a date field should always display the first day of the next month in which the program is executed. This will require a few additional steps.

Keep the cursor on the column *Selection Variable* and press "F4". From the values displayed, choose "D" denoting "Date". This will fill the Selection Variable column for the relevant fields with "D".

Next, select the F4 help of the *Name of Variable* field and choose the option "First Day of Next Month". Your Variant attributes screen will look like the one shown in Figure 6.28 for the given input field.

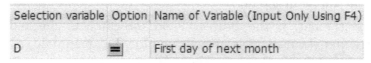

Figure 6.28: Name of Variable

> **NOTE:** The three fields will appear grey but will accept input.

6.3.3 Changing and Deleting Variants

To delete Variants, you may choose the menu path *Delete* → *Variants* and click on the appropriate row that needs to be deleted.

You may simply change a given Variant by choosing the Variant using the menu path *Variants* → *Get* or using keys "Shift+F5". This will populate the selection screen fields with the values stored in the selected Variant. Make your changes, and then choose the *Save* button.

You will then be taken to the Variant Attributes screen. You may then save changes made to the Variant. A dialog box will appear (see Figure 6.29) confirming the overwriting of the Variant in question.

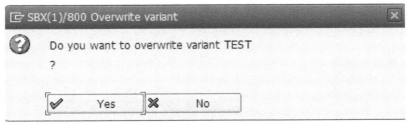

Figure 6.29: Overwrite Variant

Chapter 6 Summary

This chapter discussed the various options available to enhance your work experience with selection screens. By implementing the use of Variants, understanding how to specify single values and ranges, and mastering such components as radio buttons and single value input fields, the user should find working with selection screens to be easier and a more efficient use of time.

Chapter 7

ALV Displays

Since Release 4.6, SAP has empowered the reporting capability by providing users with the ALV data displays. The ALV data displays provide a variety of important functions to the user.

ALV will display data in either full-screen design or without it. I will begin with an explanation of both types, and then I will move on to cover the details of the various functions provided in ALV. The following topics will be covered:

- *ALV Displays,* including selecting a given column, moving columns using the mouse, and freezing columns.

- *Toolbar Functions Available,* including sorting (ascending and descending), navigating left and right, filtering data, calculating totals and subtotals, and changing views.

- *Excel Downloading,* in order to save displayed data on desktop.

- *Managing Layouts*, including change of column sequence and hiding them, if necessary.

This chapter is meant to help the user become comfortable while working within the ALV format. It will answer such questions as:

- *What are my options for different views available in ALV?*
- *How can I download my data into Excel?*
- *What are the typical functions available to me in various modes of ALV?*

Along the way, there will be examples and screen shots to make operating within ALV as easy and straightforward as possible.

7.1 ALV Displays: An Overview

ALV or **SAP/ABAP List Viewer** is a format for displaying data in reports. This format has a number of toolbar functions as well as menu options and context menu functions to assist you when carrying out useful tasks. Mastering all of these functions will help you achieve your goals in less time.

There are two types of ALV displays, namely a Full-screen display and a Container display that is not full screen (this mode is used for ALV displayed output for SAP queries).

An ALV Full-screen display is shown in Figure 7.1. The ALV data is displayed on the entire screen, and the set of ALV functions toolbar is displayed in place of the application toolbar. The ALV display may also have a header area. In Figure 7.1, the header displays the date, time, title, or company logo.

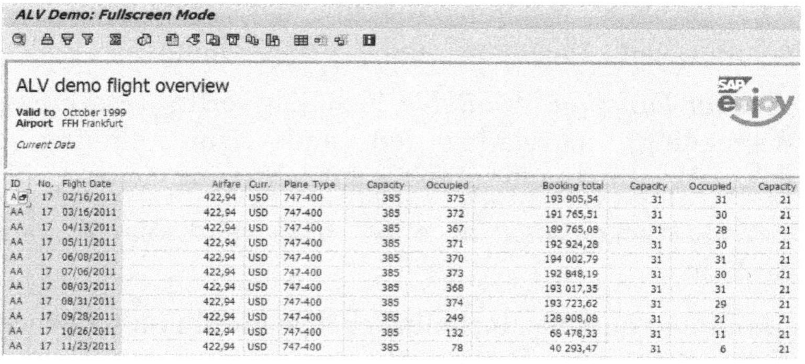

ID	No.	Flight Date	Airfare	Curr.	Plane Type	Capacity	Occupied	Booking total	Capacity	Occupied	Capacity
AA	17	02/16/2011	422,94	USD	747-400	385	375	193 905,54	31	31	21
AA	17	03/16/2011	422,94	USD	747-400	385	372	191 765,51	31	30	21
AA	17	04/13/2011	422,94	USD	747-400	385	367	189 765,08	31	28	21
AA	17	05/11/2011	422,94	USD	747-400	385	371	192 924,28	31	30	21
AA	17	06/08/2011	422,94	USD	747-400	385	370	194 002,79	31	31	21
AA	17	07/06/2011	422,94	USD	747-400	385	373	192 848,19	31	30	21
AA	17	08/03/2011	422,94	USD	747-400	385	368	193 017,35	31	31	21
AA	17	08/31/2011	422,94	USD	747-400	385	374	193 723,62	31	29	21
AA	17	09/28/2011	422,94	USD	747-400	385	249	128 908,08	31	21	21
AA	17	10/26/2011	422,94	USD	747-400	385	132	68 478,33	31	11	21
AA	17	11/23/2011	422,94	USD	747-400	385	78	40 293,47	31	6	21

Figure 7.1: ALV Full Screen Display

In some cases, each displayed row may have a corresponding checkbox for selecting any number of rows that you desire. You are also able to carry out certain actions by choosing an appropriate toolbar button. In some cases, an ALV may also have editable columns for taking input from user, but this is very rare.

An ALV may contain data columns comprised of numbers, amounts, text, and dates, as well as icons or symbols, such as traffic signals denoting the status of a record as shown in Figure 7.2. You may have ALV in single-line and multiple-line formats.

⊗○○	10002910
	10002918
	10002920
	10002922
	10002973
○△○	10002921
	10002972
	10002901
	384
	414

Figure 7.2: Signal Icons Displayed as Columns

There may also be a hotspot displayed within a list column. Clicking the hotspot may take you to the details screen for the column in question.

A list may also have key figures displayed in blue as shown in Figure 7.3.

	Cl.	PersNo	STy.	ObjID	LI	End Date	Start Date	RNo	Chngd on	Changed by	H
	800	69	0			12/31/9999	01/01/2003		09/17/2003	HOLDERM	
	800	70	0			12/31/9999	01/01/2003		09/17/2003	HOLDERM	
	800	71	0			12/31/9999	01/01/2003		09/30/2003	HOLDERM	
	800	72	0			12/31/9999	01/01/2003		09/30/2003	HOLDERM	
	800	73	0			12/31/9999	01/01/2003		09/30/2003	HOLDERM	

Figure 7.3: Key Fields Displayed in Blue

Note: In the black and white print book, the blue appears as dark gray.

Scrolling to the right will make the columns on the left appear invisible, but the key fields in blue will always remain visible, as they are fixed columns.

You have the data displayed in the form of a grid, along with a toolbar with a variety of useful functions. ALV displays may also have additional functions (buttons) specific to the application in question. The full-screen mode has a number of ALV toolbar functions as shown in Figure 7.4. The functions listed in Figure 7.4 are only available in the full-screen mode in a majority of the reports.

Q	Details	⬛	Mail
▣	Select All	⬛	Save Layout
▣	Deselect All	⊞	Change Layout
⬛	Sort Ascending	⬛	Manage Layout
⬛	Sort Descending	⬛	ABC Analysis
⬛	Filter	Σ	Total
⬛	Export	⬛	Excel Spreadsheet

Figure 7.4: ALV Toolbar Functions in Full-Screen Mode

The ALV provides a number of advantages to the user, some of which are listed below:

- Unlike typical lists, a variety of powerful functions are supported.
- You may download the reports in a number of different formats, such as Excel, Word, etc.
- You can reduce (filter) the displayed number of records by specifying filter criteria.
- Many functions, such as total and subtotals, may be performed on the number and amount fields.
- You may change the layout of displayed fields. For example, you can hide columns or change column positions and move them back and forth.
- You may also save the changes within the layout in order to use them afterwards.
- To view details of a particular column or row, you may click on a row or a hotspot within a column to view details, if applicable.
- Charts may also be generated on the basis of data displayed.

NOTE: Depending on the mode of the ALV display, the position of the toolbar may vary. The full screen display has the toolbar at the application toolbar place. In non-full-screen mode, the toolbar is within the screen details area as shown in Figure 7.5.

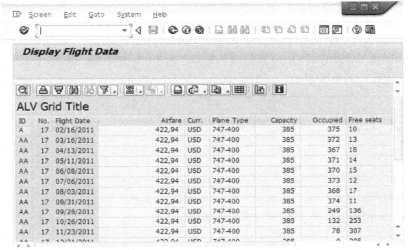

Figure 7.5: Non-Full-Screen Mode

7.1.1 Selecting a Given Column or Columns

Before moving forward, let us discuss an important feature of ALV that you need to know: selecting columns of your choice. To select an entire column in ALV, simply click the column header. This will select the column and it will appear in a grid as shown in Figure 7.6.

Cl.	PersNo	STy.	ObjID	LI	End Date	Start Date	RNo	Chngd on	Changed by	H	Tx	Rf
800	69	0			12/31/9999	01/01/2003		09/17/2003	HOLDERM			
800	70	0			12/31/9999	01/01/2003		09/17/2003	HOLDERM			
800	71	0			12/31/9999	01/01/2003		09/30/2003	HOLDERM			
800	72	0			12/31/9999	01/01/2003		09/30/2003	HOLDERM			
800	73	0			12/31/9999	01/01/2003		09/30/2003	HOLDERM			
800	1042	0			12/31/2001	01/01/1998		11/18/1998	BONIN			

Figure 7.6: Selected Columns "End Date"
and "Changed By" (in orange)

To select multiple columns, press the "CTRL" key after selecting the first column. You may then select further columns by clicking on the respective headers. (Make sure the "CTRL" key is pressed while multiple columns are selected).

7.1.2 Moving Columns and Searching for Values

Within ALV Grids, you have the option of moving columns. The columns displayed in Figure 7.7 are shown before their positions have been changed.

Start Date	Chngd on	Changed by
01/01/2003	09/17/2003	HOLDERM
01/01/2003	09/17/2003	HOLDERM
01/01/2003	09/30/2003	HOLDERM
01/01/2003	09/30/2003	HOLDERM
01/01/2003	09/30/2003	HOLDERM
01/01/1998	11/18/1998	BONIN
01/01/2002	11/18/1998	BONIN
01/01/1994	12/12/1996	MIERZWA
01/01/1998	11/18/1998	BONIN
01/01/2002	11/18/1998	BONIN

Figure 7.7: Columns Before Change

You may move the *Changed by* column to the second position (before *Changed on* column) by simply selecting it. Then, while holding the left mouse button down, drag the column to the left and place it in the second position. The new positions of the columns are shown in Figure 7.8.

Start Date	Changed by	Chngd on
01/01/2003	HOLDERM	09/17/2003
01/01/2003	HOLDERM	09/17/2003
01/01/2003	HOLDERM	09/30/2003
01/01/2003	HOLDERM	09/30/2003
01/01/2003	HOLDERM	09/30/2003
01/01/1998	BONIN	11/18/1998
01/01/2002	BONIN	11/18/1998
01/01/1994	MIERZWA	12/12/1996
01/01/1998	BONIN	11/18/1998
01/01/2002	BONIN	11/18/1998
01/01/1996	MIERZWA	12/12/1996
01/01/1998	BONIN	11/18/1998

Figure 7.8: New Positions of Columns

Within the column you may search for an entire word, a partial set of characters or a number value.

For the normal full-screen mode, select a given column and then use keys "CTRL+F" or use the menu option *Edit → Search*. You may also use the context menu option *Find*.

> **NOTE:** For non-full-screen mode, you may have an additional option toolbar 🔠 button. For the next occurrence, use the 🔠 button.

The dialog appears as shown in Figure 7.9.

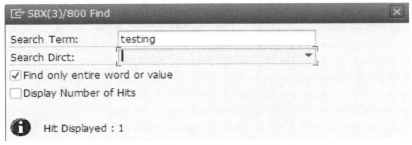

Figure 7.9: Searching Terms within a Column

Enter the search term in the dialog box (in our case "testing").

You may check the *Find only entire word or value* checkbox if that option is needed. Next, press "Enter" and the various hits will be displayed in the given column.

If the *Display Number of Hits* checkbox is unchecked, the hits are displayed one by one without the total number of occurrences of the given text in the given column as in Figure 7.10.

🗁 SBX(3)/800 Find		⊠
Search Term:	testing	
Search Dirct:	▌	▾
✔ Find only entire word or value		
☐ Display Number of Hits		
ⓘ Hit Displayed : 1		

**Figure 7.10: Search Results Displayed
Without Total Number of Occurrences**

The next hit will be displayed after pressing "Enter".

If you check the checkbox *Display Number of Hits*, the hits found will be shown as in Figure 7.11.

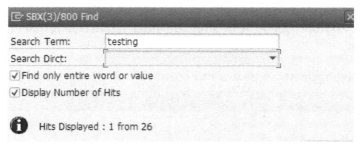

**Figure 7.11: Hits Displayed with the
"Display Number of Hits" Checkbox Selected**

With each hit that is displayed, you will be taken to the respective cell that has the match in it.

7.1.3 Freezing Columns

In any given ALV output, there may be important areas of key fields that you may want to be visible as you scroll to the right or left within the display. You may therefore freeze one or more fields of the ALV display. For freezing fields, select the given field(s) and then right-click to choose the option *Freeze to Column* (see Figure 7.12).

Clt	ID	No.	Date	Airfare	Curr	Plane	Capacity in economy class
800	AA	17	02/23/2011	422,	Copy Text		385
800	AA	17	03/23/2011	422,	Hide		385
800	AA	17	04/20/2011	422,	Show...		385
800	AA	17	05/18/2011	422,	Optimize Width		385
800	AA	17	06/15/2011	422,			385
800	AA	17	07/13/2011	422,	Freeze to Column		385
800	AA	17	08/10/2011	422,	Sort in Ascending Order		385
800	AA	17	09/07/2011	422,	Sort in Descending Order		385
800	AA	17	10/05/2011	422,	Find		385
800	AA	17	11/02/2011	422,			385
800	AA	17	11/30/2011	422,	Find Next		385
800	AA	17	12/28/2011	422,	Set Filter...		385
800	AA	17	01/25/2012	422,	Total		385
800	AA	17	02/22/2012	422,94	USD	747-400	385
800	AA	64	02/25/2011	422,94	USD	A310-300	280
800	AA	64	03/25/2011	422,94	USD	A310-300	280

Figure 7.12: Freeze to Column

All the columns from the beginning (in our case *Clt* to *Airfare*) will be frozen. If you need to unfreeze the columns, right-click anywhere on the ALV output and choose the context menu option *Unfreeze Columns*.

> **NOTE:** Copy and Pasting Values from the ALV is very easy. As with other places within the SAP system, you may also use the "CTRL+Y" keys for Copy and Paste values data displayed in one or more cells.

7.2 Toolbar Functions Available

In this section, I will take a close look at the various function buttons available in the ALV toolbar. The typical toolbar displayed in the full-screen mode is shown in Figure 7.13.

Figure 7.13: Full-Screen Mode Toolbar

On the other hand, the toolbar for the non-full-screen mode is shown in Figure 7.14.

Figure 7.14: Non-Full-Screen Mode Toolbar

Let us now discuss how to carry out some simple tasks within ALV. In this section, I will also provide the corresponding menu options for the toolbar options listed.

7.2.1 Sorting (Ascending and Descending)

You may sort the records in the ALV display either in ascending or descending order. The two buttons used for this purpose are ⬛ and ⬛ respectively.

Select a column whose criteria you need sorted in either ascending or descending order. To sort in ascending order, click the ⬛ button.

The list will appear sorted. To sort in descending order, click the ⬇ button.

If multiple columns are to be sorted, click any of the icons again. The dialog box appears as shown in Figure 7.15.

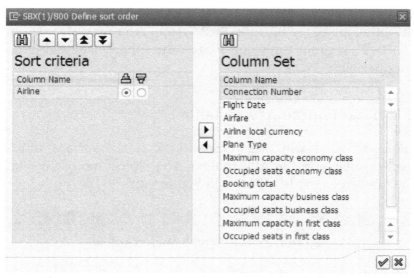

Figure 7.15: Dialog Box For Sorting Multiple Columns

Here you may use the ◀ button to add any of the fields in the column set (on the right) to the Sort criteria (or you may simply drag and drop fields to the left). You may then specify whether Ascending or Descending Sort is applicable to the Sort Criteria columns.

To go directly to the Define Sort Order dialog shown in Figure 7.15, use the menu paths *Edit → Sort in Ascending Order* or *Sort in Descending Order*.

7.2.2 Navigating Left and Right

If you are in the ALV list output mode (discussed in the section 7.2.5.4 "Print Preview/ List Output" ahead), and the columns within the ALV list are more than the visible width of the screen, you may scroll left and right using the ◀ and ▶ navigation buttons respectively.

The key fields/frozen fields will not disappear despite the scrolling. To go to the end of the list to the extreme right, use the ▶| button. To go to the extreme left, use the |◀ button.

7.2.3 Filtering Data

ALV reporting also gives you the power to filter data according to your own defined criteria. You may define the criteria using one or more fields (and their values) displayed in the ALV. For example, if the Salary column is there in your output, you may set the filter in order to display salaries ranging from $10,000 to $ 20,000.

There are two steps involved when defining Filters:

- You specify the fields that are to be used for defining the filtering.

- Then you specify the values for the filter-specific fields.

Simply click the *Filter* button 🔽 on the ALV toolbar. The dialog box appears as shown in Figure 7.16.

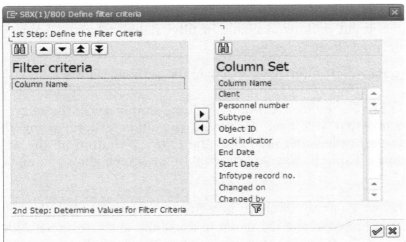

Figure 7.16: Defining Filter Criteria

On the right side, all of the columns appearing in the ALV will be listed. You may select a field or multiple fields and use the ◀ button to bring them to the left side, thus defining the filter criteria. You may also drag and drop fields from the right side to the left instead of using the mouse.

Next, you need to specify values for the filter criteria. For this, click on the ▼ icon shown at the bottom of the screen. The dialog appears as shown in Figure 7.17.

Figure 7.17: Determine Values for Filter Criteria

A range of selection criteria appears for each input field selected. Enter the values for the criteria. For more information on the various input options available in filter fields, refer to Chapter 6 - Mastering Selection Screens.

The data will be filtered according to the defined criteria.

> **NOTE:** For quick definition of filters, simply select the relevant column that you need to use in the Filter criteria using the column header, and then click the *Filter* ▼ button on the ALV toolbar. This will take you directly to the screen shown in Figure 7.17.

> **NOTE:** To apply filters in non-full-screen mode, click the ▼ button to access the list menu options and choose the *Set Filter* option from the menu that appears (see Figure 7.18).

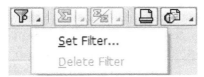

Figure 7.18: Set Filter Option

7.2.4 Calculating Totals, Subtotals, and Averages

If at least a single number, amount field, or quantity appears in the display, the *Total* Σ button is visible and enabled on the toolbar. If you want to total a particular column, select the column by clicking on the column header and then click on the *Total* Σ button. This will total the column, and the totals will appear in yellow as shown in Figure 7.19.

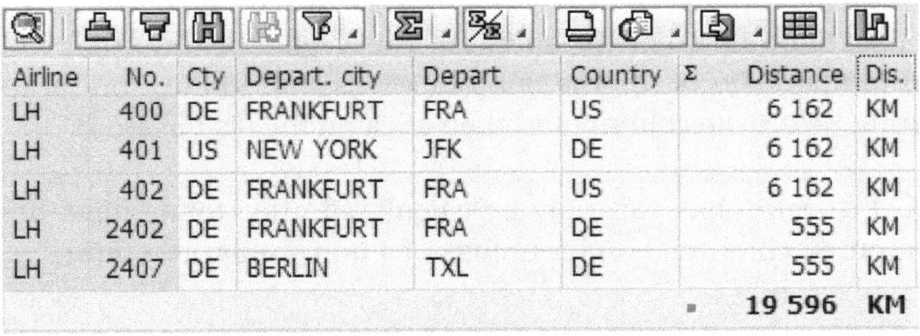

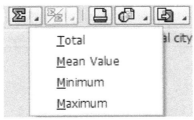

Airline	No.	Cty	Depart. city	Depart	Country Σ	Distance	Dis.
LH	400	DE	FRANKFURT	FRA	US	6 162	KM
LH	401	US	NEW YORK	JFK	DE	6 162	KM
LH	402	DE	FRANKFURT	FRA	US	6 162	KM
LH	2402	DE	FRANKFURT	FRA	DE	555	KM
LH	2407	DE	BERLIN	TXL	DE	555	KM
						19 596	KM

Figure 7.19: Total Displayed for Distance

For non-full-screen mode, the toolbar button is shown in Figure 7.20.

Figure 7.20: Total Button in Non-Full-Screen Mode

This button comes with four functions that are accessed via a list menu. The functions are *Total, Mean Value, Minimum*, and *Maximum*.

To access a particular function, choose the relevant option, such as Minimum, Maximum, etc. The relevant function will then be applied to the chosen column, and the result will be shown in yellow as seen in Figure 7.21.

LH 🗗	400	DE	FRANKFURT	FRA	US	6 162	KM
LH	401	US	NEW YORK	JFK	DE	6 162	KM
LH	402	DE	FRANKFURT	FRA	US	6 162	KM
LH	2402	DE	FRANKFURT	FRA	DE	555	KM
LH	2407	DE	BERLIN	TXL	DE	555	KM
					▪	3 919,20	KM

Figure 7.21: Average Value Computed for Distance

In the above figure, the average of the distance is calculated.

Suppose the totaling has been done for an ALV output; you may also compute subtotals. For the subtotal, you need a column that will be used as the criteria for the subtotal. This must be a non-numeric column. Select the column and then click on the ⅗ button.

NOTE: Subtotals can only be calculated after totals have been computed and based on groupings of a non-numeric column.

This will calculate the subtotals as well. In the following figure, the Airline column values are used as the basis of the Subtotaling.

Airline	No.	Flight Date	Σ	Capacity
AA	17	02/15/2012		31
	64	02/18/2011		22
	64	03/18/2011		22
	64	04/15/2011		22
	64	05/13/2011		22
	64	06/10/2011		22
	64	07/08/2011		22
	64	08/05/2011		22
	64	09/02/2011		22
	64	09/30/2011		22
	64	10/28/2011		22
	64	11/25/2011		22
	64	12/23/2011		22
	64	01/20/2012		22
	64	02/17/2012		22
AA	⛁		▪	**742**
AZ	555	02/16/2011		22
	555	03/16/2011		22
AZ	⛁		▪	**44**
⛁			▪▪	**786**

Figure 7.22: Calculating Subtotals

As shown in Figure 7.22, the subtotals of the Capacity column are calculated for the Airlines. The Airline AA has a subtotal (total capacity) of 742, and AZ has a capacity of 44. Finally, the grand total is shown at the end of the line. The subtotals appear highlighted in a light yellow color.

You may condense the subtotal details of a particular Airline by clicking the ⛁ icon.

You may have different views for Subtotals calculation. Choose the menu option *Settings → Define Drill Down Options*. The dialog box in our case for Airline subtotals appears as shown in Figure 7.23.

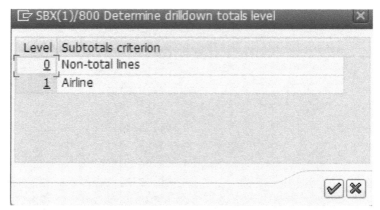

Figure 7.23: Airline Subtotals Dialog Box

Choose the *1 - Airline* criterion and press "Enter". Your entire display will appear in condensed form showing only the Capacity totals for each Airline as shown in Figure 7.24.

Airline	▲	No.	Flight Date	Σ	Capacity
AA				▪	**742**
AZ				▪	**44**
				▪▪	**786**

Figure 7.24: Capacity Totals For Each Airline

To switch back to the expanded form showing all of the data (as shown in Figure 7.22), choose the *0 - Non-total lines* criterion.

7.2.5 Changing Views

One important feature of the ALV is to display your data into different views. In this section we will discuss three views: **Excel Inplace View**, **Charts View**, and **ABC Analysis Function View**. We will also discuss how you can display your data in Print Preview or List Output.

7.2.5.1 Excel Inplace View

One popular view is the Excel Inplace view. With this, the toolbar is visible but the grid display is replaced with an Excel view embedded on your SAP screen as shown in Figure 7.25.

> **NOTE:** A setting needs to be switched on for the Excel Inplace to run correctly. From Excel applications, choose the menu option *File → Options*. From the dialog box that appears, choose *Trust Center* from the left pane. Then, click the *Trust Center Settings* button. Make sure Macro Settings are selected from the left pane (see Figure 7.25). On the screen, make sure the checkbox for *Trust access to the VBA project Object Model* under the Developer Macro Settings is switched on.

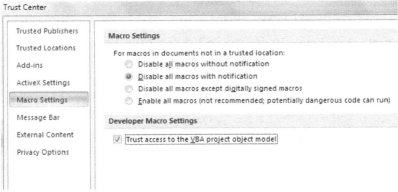

Figure 7.25: Trust Center Macro Settings

For a full-screen mode, once the Excel Inplace view is chosen, the screen display will change as shown in Figure 7.26.

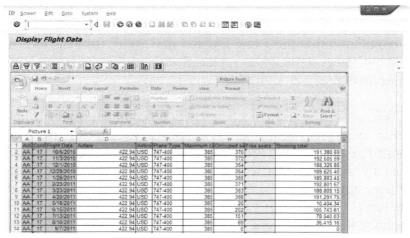

Figure 7.26: Excel View Shown With ALV Output

7.2.5.2 Generating Charts View

You may also generate charts and other useful graphics using your choice of the data displayed in the ALV. By simply selecting different columns, you can generate a variety of chart outputs for a particular ALV data.

> NOTE: Charts may be generated based on the selected columns or after groupings performed in Subtotal calculation.

To generate charts, simply select the columns that you need to show in graphic form and then press the ▦ button. (Alternately, you may choose the menu path *Views→ Graphic*.) A new ALV Graphic window will appear showing the chart. You may right-click the chart and send a print.

Suppose we have calculated the Airline wise subtotal of the Capacity column as shown in Figures 7.22 and 7.23, and then clicked the ▦ button; the corresponding chart will be generated as shown in Figure 7.27.

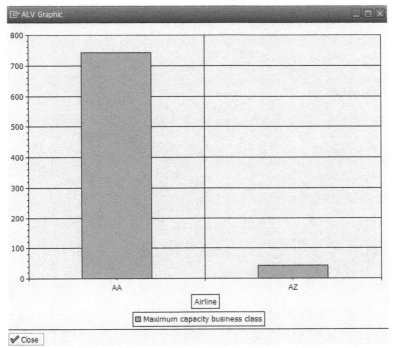

Figure 7.27: Capacity of Airline Subtotals Generated as a Chart

7.2.5.3 ABC Analysis Function View

The **ABC Analysis** function lets you divide the data into three (or even two) portions. There are four analysis types available; the most important of which is Key Figure Percent. This allows you to divide data based on the specified percentages A, B, and C. The percentage of the A, B, and C may be set. For example, A may be set as 70%, B as 20%, and C as 10%. Part A constitutes the most important part of the data. Part B is less important. Part C is the least important.

To carry out the ABC analysis, select the numeric column you are interested in (in our case, Bookings Total) and click the 📊 button. This will take you to the screen shown in Figure 7.28 showing the ABC Analysis results. By default, the Key Figure Percent type is applicable and the values of A, B, and C are 70%, 20%, and 10% respectively. You may change the values according to your needs and then press "Enter".

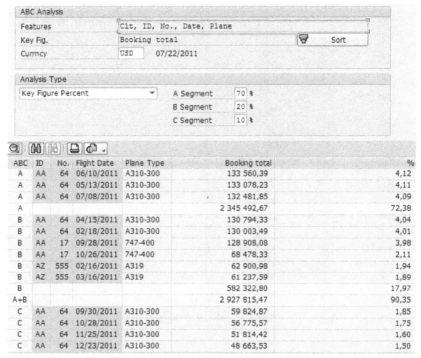

Figure 7.28 ABC Analysis Results

The lower portion shows the results of the Analysis. The values for A, B, and C segments we chose divide the list into three parts:

- the set of rows which form approximately 70 percent of the entire bookings totals (A Segment, see Figure 7.28)

- the set of rows which form 20 percent of the bookings total (B Segment)

- the remaining 10 percent (C Segment)

By default, the list is sorted in descending order, which means that the rows that have the highest value of Bookings form the Segment A and so on. In case you want to sort the list in ascending order, click the 🌪 Sort button or choose the menu option *Edit → Sort*.

7.2.5.4 Print Preview/ List Output

In addition to the ALV Grid format, you have the option of displaying the print preview of the data in ALV list format. For this, click on the ⎙ button. Alternately, you may use the menu option *List → Print Preview*. This will change the output as shown in Figure 7.29.

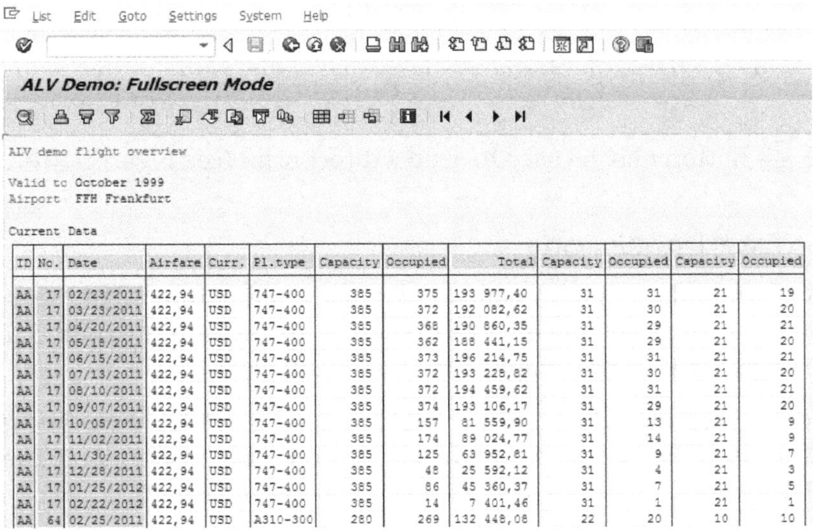

Figure 7.29: ALV List Format Output

You may send the print from here by choosing the menu option *List → Print*. For the non-full-screen mode, you may click the ⎙ button to access the available options as shown in Figure 7.30. Then choose the *List Output* option.

159

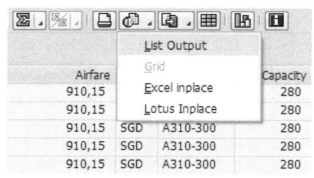

Figure 7.30: List Output Option

The 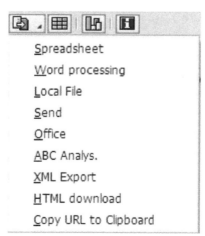 button may be used to send a direct print (see Figure 7.30).

7.2.6 Excel Downloading

ALV format lets you download displayed data into a number of formats. A popular download for users is to save the work in Excel. The steps for Excel download are shown below.

To download into Excel in the non-full-screen mode, click the ⬜ button and choose the Spreadsheet option from the context menu that appears.

Figure 7.31: Context Menu in Non-Full-Screen Mode

Next, you will be presented with two options: *Table* and *Pivot table*. Choose the option *Table*. It will take you to the dialog box as shown in Figure 7.32.

Figure 7.32: Choosing "Excel" Download

You may then be asked to confirm Microsoft Excel as your format. After this, press the "Enter" button.

NOTE: Any calculated applied filters, totals, and subtotals are simply ignored in the Excel download. If the list is too long, an error is displayed and no download is performed.

An Excel window will open and show the data as shown in Figure 7.33.

	A	B	C	D	E	F	G	H	I	J	K
1	ID	No.	Plane Type	Free seats	Date	Airfare	Curr.	Capacity	Occupied	Booking total	Capacity
2	AA	17	747-400	15	40457	422.94	USD	385	370	191,380.59	191380.
3	AA	17	747-400	13	40485	422.94	USD	385	372	192,505.59	192505.
4	AA	17	747-400	21	40513	422.94	USD	385	364	188,326.85	188326.
5	AA	17	747-400	21	40541	422.94	USD	385	364	189,625.40	18962!
6	AA	17	747-400	20	40569	422.94	USD	385	365	189,883.45	189883.
7	AA	17	747-400	14	40597	422.94	USD	385	371	192,801.67	192801.
8	AA	17	747-400	22	40625	422.94	USD	385	363	188,809.15	188809.
9	AA	17	747-400	17	40653	422.94	USD	385	368	191,291.75	191291.
10	AA	17	747-400	365	40681	422.94	USD	385	20	10,404.34	10404.
11	AA	17	747-400	183	40709	422.94	USD	385	202	105,743.61	105743.
12	AA	17	747-400	234	40737	422.94	USD	385	151	78,540.03	78540.
13	AA	17	747-400	316	40765	422.94	USD	385	69	36,415.16	36415.
14	AA	17	747-400	385	40793	422.94	USD	385	0	0.00	
15	AA	17	747-400	385	40821	422.94	USD	385	0	0.00	

Figure 7.33: Excel Worksheet

You may also convert data into a Pivot table format. For this, instead of Table option, choose *Pivot table*.

7.2.7 Managing Layouts

Apart from other useful functions, you may also change the layout of the fields within the display. In ALV you may change the sequence as well as hide fields (columns) and save your layout for the next execution of the report. As already mentioned, you may set the filters according to the given criteria, sort fields, as well as change the sequence of the displayed data. The layout includes any added filter as well as gives you the facility of saving the layout for future use.

To change the layout, click the ▦ button on the toolbar. This will display the *Change Layout* dialog box as shown in Figure 7.34.

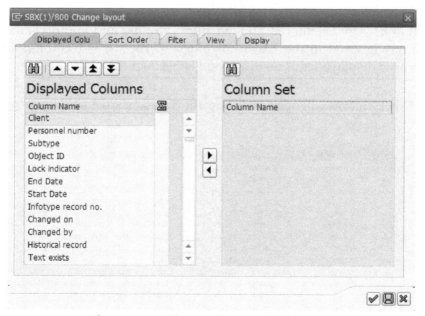

Figure 7.34: Change Layout Dialog Box

You will be presented with a number of tabs that will allow you to hide certain columns of your choice or specify the Sort Order and the Filter criteria.

The first tab is for the *Displayed Columns* (see Figure 7.35).

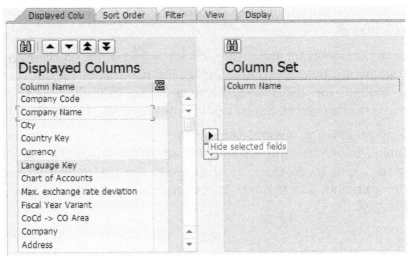

Figure 7.35: Displayed Columns

On the left side are the columns that are currently displayed. If you wish to hide any columns, they must be selected and transferred to the right block labeled *Column Set*.

> **NOTE:** For the non-full-screen mode, press the ⊞ ⌄ button to access the menu. Then choose the *Change Layout* option.

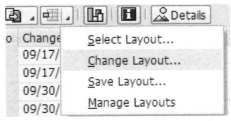

Figure 7.36: Change Layout Option

You may select one or more fields using the "CTRL" key and then click the ▶ button to hide the fields selected. In the Figure 7.35, the Company name and Language Key will be removed from the display. You may also specify the Sort criteria and the Filter criteria using the *Sort Order* and *Filter* tabs respectively. When you press "Enter", the data will appear changed according to the changed Layout specifications.

To save the layout for the future, click the ⊟ button on the *Change Layout* popup box. Alternately, you may use the ⊞ button on the ALV toolbar for the non-full-screen mode. Simply choose this button and click on the *Save Layout* option.

To load an existing layout, click on the ⊞ button. From the list of options, choose the appropriate layout. If no layouts exists, the message ☑ No layouts found is displayed. For the non-full-screen mode, you may use the menu option Select Layout as shown in Figure 7.36.

Summary of Chapter 7

This chapter discussed the various functions found within the ALV format. With the information in this chapter, you should now be able to select columns, move columns with the mouse, and freeze various columns. You should also be comfortable with the toolbar functions within both the full-screen and non-full-screen modes.

Chapter 8

Printing Guide

No matter how paperless an environment becomes, printing remains an important part of the working life of an SAP user. The purpose of this chapter is to introduce you to the printing options available within SAP.

This chapter will cover the following important topics:

- *Printing window contents*
- *Printing from report selection screens*
- *Form Printing*
- *Changing the look and feel of print dialog*
- *PDF creations from spool requests*
- *Print-related problems*

Since printing is such an important activity for the SAP user, this chapter will detail how you can directly print a report out and send the contents directly to the printer. Related to this, we will have a look at the Print Immediately and Send to Spool request options for everyday printing.

Some questions that will be answered in this chapter include:

- *How can I print an entire screenshot of my current SAP session?*
- *How do I create Spool Requests?*
- *What are the different Spool Request Attributes?*
- *How can I convert Spool Requests to PDFs?*

Throughout the chapter, there will be examples and screenshots to help the reader understand the printing process.

8.1 Quick Hard Copy

A simple way to print the entire screenshot of the current SAP session without encountering any dialog box is to use the **Hard Copy** option. This sends the screen's print to the default printer of your PC. It will send it directly without asking for any information. This action takes a snapshot of the entire SAP screen. To choose this function, proceed as follows:

- Click the *Customizing Layout* button on the standard toolbar. The menu will appear as shown in Figure 8.1.

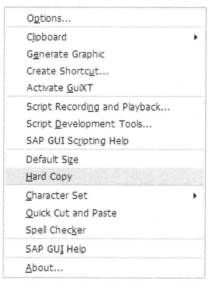

Figure 8.1: Customizing Layout Menu

Choose the *Hard Copy* option. This will send a print to the default printer immediately.

8.2 Printing Window Contents

To send a print of the SAP screen content, such as a list, a form, or an ALV output, you may choose the *Print* option by clicking the 🖨 button. Alternately, you may also use the keys "CTRL+P".

The dialog box then appears as shown in Figure 8.2.

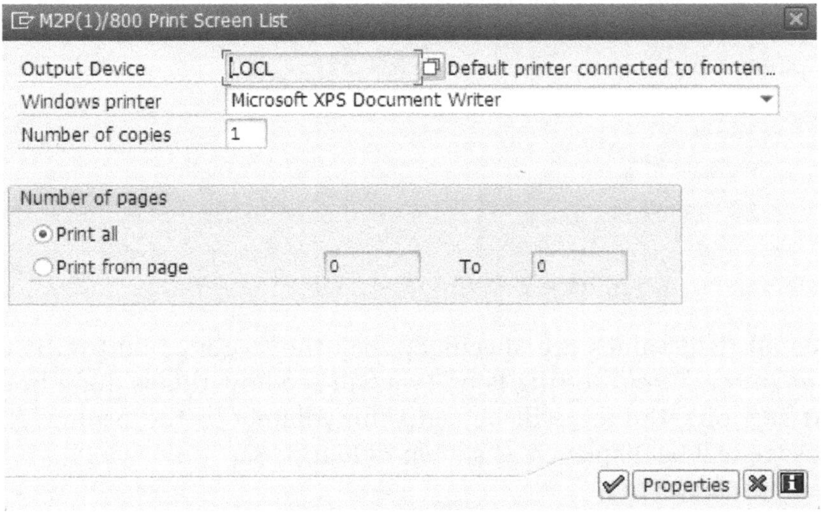

Figure 8.2: Print Screen List

The important fields on this screen are shown below:

- *Output Device:* This is the name of the printer as defined within the SAP system. You may choose the F4 help to display a list of defined output devices. If you choose LOCL or LOCAL, your print will be sent directly to the default printer connected to your PC.

- *Windows/frontend Printer:* This is a dropdown list that allows you to choose from the printers connected to your PC. Choose a suitable printer from the dropdown list.

- *Number of Copies:* By default, this field contains the value "1". If you would like to print multiple copies, enter the desired number in this field.

- *Number of Pages:* You may also select the number of pages that you require. By default, the *Print all* option for Number of Pages is selected. Selecting *Print all* will print all the pages of the list or form (no matter if they are 100 or 1000). In case you want to print only a certain page range of the list or form, select the radio button *Print from Page...to...* The *From* and *To* page number fields will be enabled as shown in Figure 6.3. You may then enter the range you desire to print. For example, we printed pages 1 to 5.

Number of pages

○ Print all

◉ Print from page   1   To   5

Figure 8.3: Number of Pages to Print

Once all field values are specified, click the ☑ Enter button. If the *Print Immediately* setting is on (we will see how this is done in the next section), the job will be sent immediately to the printer. The message will be displayed as shown in Figure 8.4.

☑ Spool request (number 0000035231) sent to SAP printer LOCL

Figure 8.4: Printer Message

However, if we have set the option *Sent to Spool*, a Spool request will be created and no immediate output is sent (see message in Figure 8.5). We will see how the attributes may be set in the next section.

☑ Spool request (number 0000035315) created without immediate output

Figure 8.5: No Immediate Output

If you choose the *Without Immediate Output* option, a Spool request is created and may be viewed using the transaction "SP02". Alternately, you may use menu path *System → Own Spool Requests*. The screen appears as shown in Figure 8.6.

Output Controller: List of Spool Requests

Spool no.	Type	Date	Time	Status	Pages	Title
35315		04/29/2011	13:24	-	1	LIST1S LOCL DEMO_LISTSTU
35230		04/27/2011	14:04	-	1	LIST1S LOCL DEMO_SELESTU
33256		03/08/2011	19:57	-	1	LIST1S LOCL 110308
21167		06/14/2010	05:31	-	3	LIST1S LOCL RAJAWE00_STU
21002		06/11/2010	16:47	-	2	LIST1S LOCL RAJABS00_STU
21001		06/11/2010	16:46	-	2	LIST1S LOCL RAJABS00_STU
21000		06/11/2010	16:45	-	2	LIST1S LOCL RAJABS00_STU
20991		06/11/2010	13:24	-	2	LIST1S LOCL RAJABS00_STU
20990		06/11/2010	13:22	-	3	LIST1S LOCL RAJAWE00_STU
20975		06/11/2010	07:37	-	3	LIST1S LOCL RAJAWE00_STU
17174		04/14/2010	05:43	-	4	LVS2 LOCL STUDENT008
17173		04/14/2010	05:43	-	1	LVS2 LP01 STUDENT008
17112		04/13/2010	06:59	-	1	LVS2 LP01 STUDENT008

```
13 Spool requests displayed
=====================================================================
13 Spool requests without output request
```

Figure 8.6: List of Spool Requests

This will list the entire Spool requests that you have created. Each print job sent without immediate output is stored here under a unique Spool Number. The type (ABAP list or forms) is also displayed along with the date, time, and the number of pages included in the print job. Listed in Figure 8.7 are the various types of Spool requests and their symbols.

Symbol	Type
	ABAP List (Report Output)
	Smartforms Form Output
	Adobe Forms

Figure 8.7: Types of Spool Requests

At the end of the list, you will have lines showing the total number of Spool requests displayed, as well as the total number of requests for which outputs have NOT been generated.

You may select a given Spool (or multiple Spool requests using checkboxes) and click the *Print Directly* button on the toolbar. This will send the job to the printer and the number of pages will be printed. However, if you would like to print with some changes in the spool parameters, you may do so by clicking the *Print with Changed Parameters* 🖨 button. This allows you to change certain parameters as shown in Figure 8.8.

Figure 8.8: Print Parameters

You may, for example, change the Output device and the number of copies. Moreover, you may specify the Start Date and Time for printing. When you have entered the appropriate values, you may click the *Print* button on the screen (for single values) or *Print All* button if multiple Spool requests were selected.

To delete Spool requests manually, you may select the request and then click the *Delete* button.

To display the contents of a particular Spool request, select the request and then click the *Display Contents* 👓 button. Alternately, you may press "F6" or select the Type symbol of the given Spool request. The content will then be displayed. You may also download the content of a Spool request in the form of a text file or a number of other formats (rich text format [RTF], Excel, or HTML formats), if required. Once the contents are displayed, you may choose the menu path *System → List → Save → File*. You may then specify the format and save the spool content on your local PC.

NOTE: When using the transaction SP02, you may also display output of Adobe Forms in PDF formats.

8.3 "Execute and Print" From Report Selection Screen

On report selection screens, it is also possible to execute and print the output together in one direct step. For this, choose the menu option *Execute and Print* as shown in Figure 8.9.

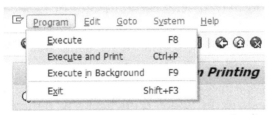

Figure 8.9: Menu Option "Execute and Print"

A Print Dialog will appear and it will look the same as the one shown in Figure 8.2. You may then specify the settings as usual in order to generate the Spool request.

8.4 Form Printing

In addition to reports, the SAP system also allows you to print forms output (both Smartforms and Adobe forms output). If you try to print forms, you will see the dialog box shown in Figure 8.10.

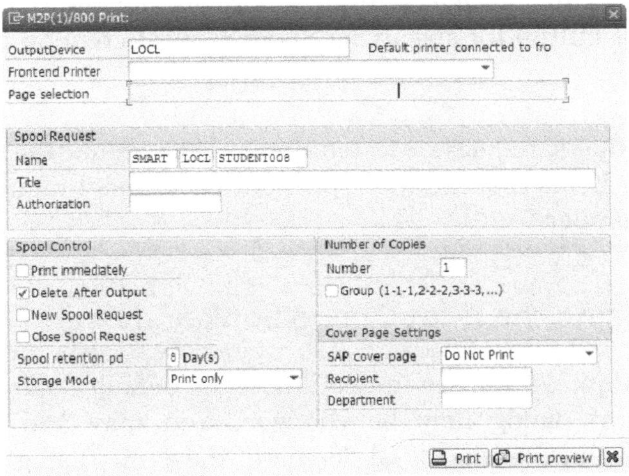

Figure 8.10: Form Printing Dialog Box

In addition to the parameters discussed previously, there exist other parameters on the dialog that are also important. Let us now go through them:

- *Page Selection.* The form output may have a number of pages. You may not need the entire set of pages to be printed. If this is the case, you may specify certain pages or range of pages from the given output to be sent to the spool system. For example, you may specify the pages "1, 2, 4-6".

- *Print Immediately.* To send the output to the printer immediately, select the *Print Immediately* checkbox. To send Spool requests to the Spooler, uncheck this indicator.

- *New Spool Request.* Checking this creates a new Spool request for your form print job.

- *Delete After Output.* If this checkbox is on, the created Spool request will be retained only until the Spool request contents have been printed.

- *Close Spool Request.* If this is on, the Spool request created will be closed and no further print jobs may use it. If this checkbox is not checked, subsequent print jobs may be added in the spool request and may be printed later all together.

There is a *Print Preview* button for previewing the output and a direct *Print* button for specifying Spool request creation or to print immediately.

> **NOTE:** Spool requests are temporary documents that contain the user's items that are to be printed. Each Spool request has a unique number.

8.5 Changing the Print Dialog Look and Feel

In this section, we will see in detail how the default fields displayed on the Print dialog may be changed. You may add up to 10 additional values to the Initial Screen of the Print Dialog (shown in Figure 8.2). Let us take a closer look at how this may be done.

On the Print Dialog, click the *Properties* button. This will lead you to the screen shown in Figure 8.11.

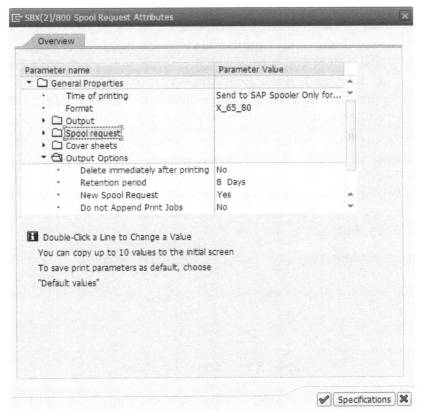

Figure 8.11: Spool Request Attributes

This screen provides you with a list of Spool request properties (attributes). As already mentioned, you can transfer up to 10 attributes to the Print Dialog. Let us now discuss some of the important ones:

- *Time of Printing.* As mentioned in the previous section, if the Time of printing is set to "Immediately" then the document is printed immediately. However, there are also two other options that may be chosen. These are shown below:

1. *Send to SAP Spooler for now.* This setting allows you to prevent sending the document to the printer immediately. When this setting is chosen, a Spool request is created that may be viewed later and printed using transaction SP01.

2. *Print Later.* This option allows you to print the document at a later date and is time specific. When you select *Print Later* a date and time field appears. You may then fill in appropriate values. This option will not work for documents sent to printers connected with your PC (frontend printing).

- *Format.* This attribute resembles the format in which the ABAP list is to be printed. You may specify the columns (width) and rows (height) to be printed on a given page. You may choose an appropriate format using the F4 help of the format field. For example, 65 rows and 80 columns are used for the format "X_65_80".

Figure 8.12: Format Attribute

Along with the above-listed attributes, a few more important ones are listed under *Output Options*. Let us have a closer look.

- *Delete Immediately after Printing.* As the name suggests, this attribute allows you to delete the created Spool request from the system once the request has been printed.

- *Retention Period.* This attribute allows you to specify a period until which the Spool request is to be retained. After this time, the Spool request will be deleted from the system and will no longer be accessible via SP01 transaction.

For each of the attributes mentioned, the value may be changed by double-clicking the attribute in question (see Figure 8.13).

Parameter name	Parameter Value
▾ 🗇 General Properties	
• Time of printing	Send to SAP Spooler Only for Now
• Format	X_65_80

Figure 8.13: Selecting an Attribute

The lower part of the screen will then display the editable attribute along with a possible set of values. For example, if you select *Time of Printing*, the editable list box appears as shown in Figure 8.14

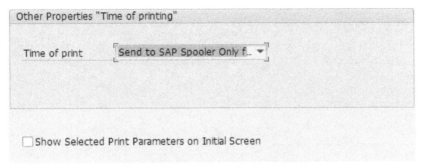

Figure 8.14: Editable Attribute

For the *Time of Print* attribute, you may choose from the options, "Send to SAP Spooler Only for Now", "Print Immediately", or "Print Later".

- *New Spool Request.* If this indicator is checked, a new Spool request will be created for the document in question. However, if you would like an existing Spool request previously created by you to be used, you should uncheck this option.

- *Do not Append Print Jobs.* If this value is set to "Yes", then no further print jobs are added to the Spool request in question. However, if this value is set to "No", then the subsequent print jobs/documents will be added to the current Spool request. This attribute may be used in conjunction with the *New Spool Request* attribute. If the former and the latter are set to "No" then all print jobs may be accumulated in one Spool request. So from SP01, you may choose one Spool request to print the entire run, thus saving you time.

Also important is a checkbox that is visible at the end of the screen with the label Show *Selected Print Parameters on Initial Screen* (see Figure 8.14). For example, if we select this indicator for the *New Spool Request* attribute, the initial dialog will display the given attribute as shown in the Print Dialog in Figure 8.15.

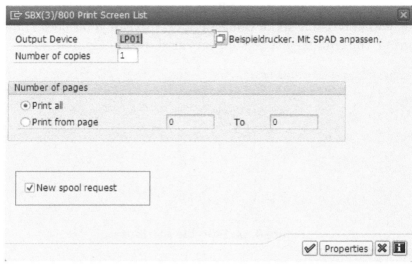

Figure 8.15: Attribute "New Spool Request" Added

8.6 Using RSTXPDFT4 Program to Convert Spool Requests to PDFs

This section will discuss how a PDF file may be generated using a Spool request number and a standard SAP program RSTXPDFT4. For this, we assume that the Spool request for the print job has already been created and exists in transaction SP01. You should note down the number for the given Spool request.

Go to transaction "SA38". Enter the name of the program RSTXPDFT4 in the *Program* field and click the *Execute* button. The selection screen of the program appears as shown in Figure 8.16.

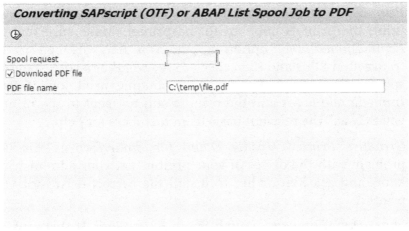

Figure 8.16: Selection Screen for Program RSTXPDFT4

Enter the Spool request number in the field shown. Make sure the *Download PDF file* checkbox is selected. You may give a suitable path for where the file is to be stored on your PC.

Next, click the *Execute* button. A *Save As* dialog box will appear showing the path for storing the generated file. You may change these values at this stage as well. Finally, click the *Save* button.

A log will be displayed regarding the generating of the PDF file from the Spool request.

8.7 Printing-Related Problems

In this section, we will discuss the typical problems you may face when printing. (There may be some issues that may be related to the printer settings.) Let us discuss them one by one.

> **NOTE:** Sometimes, when you try to open transaction Sp01 using the *Own Spool Requests* menu option, a dialog box appears stating *Maximum number of sessions reached*. If this is the case, close one session and try the transaction Sp01 again.

- *Print Not Sent.* A common problem may be that when you try to print, the print is not sent to the printer. Make sure that the *Print Immediately* option is set. You may also go to the transaction SP01 and then check to see whether a corresponding spool request exists for the corresponding print job. If *Print Immediately* is set and the print is still not sent to the printer, you may ask the relevant basis team members for help.

- *Graphics Printed Upside Down for Smartforms.* This is a problem with the driver of your printer. Let your administrator know and ask him or her to install the correct driver for your printer.

- *Short Dump appears saying Spool Buffer Full.* If this problem occurs, the most probable reason is that the spool buffer is full and no more spool requests could be allocated to your request. This problem can be fixed by the basis team members.

Summary of Chapter 8

This chapter outlined the Printing Guide for SAP users. With the information provided, you should now, among other things, be able to print window contents, print from report selection screens, change the look and feel of print dialog, convert spool requests to PDFs, and troubleshoot any printing problems that may arise.

Chapter 9

Creating Your Own Reports

This chapter will focus on SAP Query and the ways in which it will let the user generate reports based on their own data and particular needs. It places the power in the hands of the user to generate reports that are tailored to specific needs and purposes. I will discuss, in detail, the need for creating SAP Queries and how this tool can help you generate your own reports based on your unique data. The following topics will be covered:

- *Generating Basic Lists, the three types of reports that can be generated, and a step by step account of how to generate a Basic list*

- *Adding Control Levels to your list*

- *Adding a Header to your list*

- *How to add a footer to a Basic List*

Queries are a very diverse and large topic, but in this chapter, I will only cover the topics that are of interest and of use to a user. This chapter is meant to be a guide for the basic setup and use of SAP Queries. Some questions that will be answered in this chapter include:

- *How do I create a Query?*
- *What are the three types of reports that can be generated by using SAP Query?*
- *How can I add control levels to a Basic List?*

Throughout the chapter, there will be examples and screenshots to help the reader gain the greatest possible understanding of how to generate their own Queries.

9.1 SAP Query: An Overview

The **SAP Query** is a tool that allows you to generate your own reports based upon data stored into the SAP system. You do not need to rely on the services of an ABAP developer for it. You may generate your report output in a number of formats, such as ALV, simple list, graphics, etc. SAP query also allows you to define your own list of headers and footers as well as define column headings.

Before creating a Query, there are certain prerequisites that must be created. These prerequisites include an **Infoset** and **User Group**. An Infoset is the data source from which the data is to be read and displayed in your Query. A user group is the group of users that can create and change queries of a particular functional area. Both of these must exist before you can commence your Query.

You may generate three types of reports through the use of SAP Query. The three reports are **Basic List**, **Statistics**, and **Ranked Lists**. Let us discuss them one by one.

- *Basic List:* A Basic List lets you generate simple lists consisting of single or multiple lines. You may also define list headers. A Basic List with control levels may also be created for displaying the subtotals based on a certain criteria. With control levels, you may specify the field(s) based on which list is to be sorted or which totals are to be calculated.

- *Statistics:* In the case of Statistics, you can define statistical values — computed from a particular set of data. These statistical values include calculated values, such as totals, percentages, averages, etc. In other words, Statistics is a summarized form of a larger set of data. For example, you may generate a Statistics report based on Airline Codes or Department Names.

- *Ranked List:* Ranked List is a list that is sorted according to the value of a computed Statistical value. For example, Statistical value such as a Ranked List with top 20 average values.

9.2 Generating Basic Lists

In this section, I will discuss the detailed steps required to create a Basic List through the SAP Query tool.

> **NOTE:** We will print a list of airline data that will be comprised of the columns Airline code, Flight Number, Plane Type, and the Total Booking Amount of a Flight with relevant currency. We will assume that the Infoset and the User group are also created.

In order to generate a Basic List using SAP Query, proceed as follows:

- Call transaction "SQ01". The screen appears as shown in Figure 9.1.

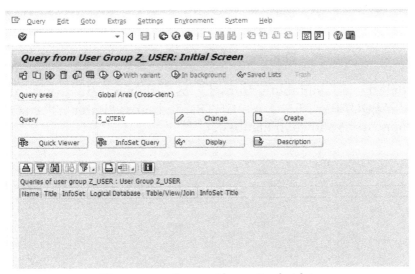

Figure 9.1: Generating a Basic List

Make sure that the correct user group is chosen. To go into the correct user group, choose the menu path *Edit → Other User Group.* A dialog box appears showing the various User Groups. Select the appropriate group and click the ✔ Choose button. This will bring you back to the screen shown in Figure 9.1 but with the title including your chosen User Group.

- Enter a suitable name for your Query in the field provided and choose *Create.* A dialog box appears as shown in Figure 9.2.

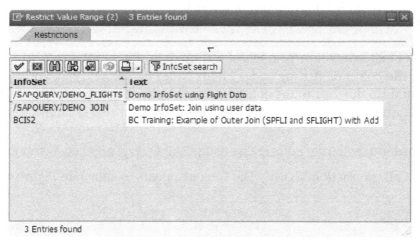

Figure 9.2: Infoset Selection

- Select a suitable Infoset as shown (in our case, /SAPQUERY/DEMO_FLIGHTS), and press "Enter". The screen appears as shown in Figure 9.3.

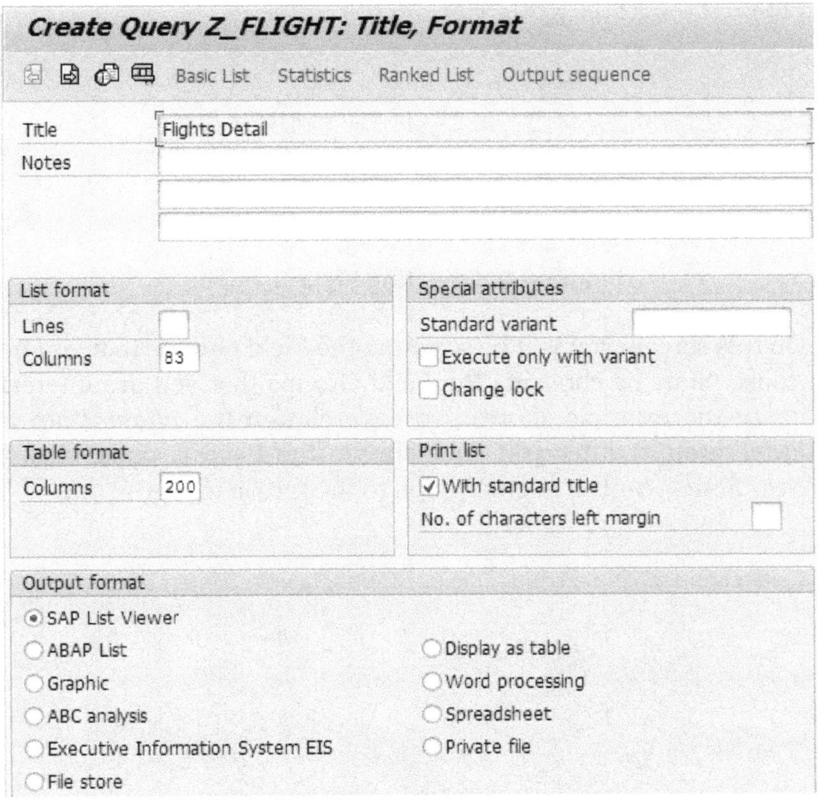

Figure 9.3: Entering Title and Description

- On the screen that appears, enter a suitable Title in the field provided. You can also define a suitable output format at this time. You may choose the default output format, such as SAP List Viewer, the simple ABAP list, Graphics, etc. You may also specify the Lines and Columns of the output in case the ABAP list is selected.

Then, click the *Next Screen* 🔄 button (or press "F6"). This takes you to the screen shown in Figure 9.4.

183

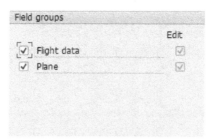

Figure 9.4: Selecting Field Groups

- On this screen, you will be selecting the Field Groups that you need to use. Start by choosing the Field Groups that you are interested in. In the example shown, we have chosen the *Flight Data* and *Plane* groups. After you have chosen the Field Groups, click the *Next Screen* button to go through to the screen in Figure 9.5.

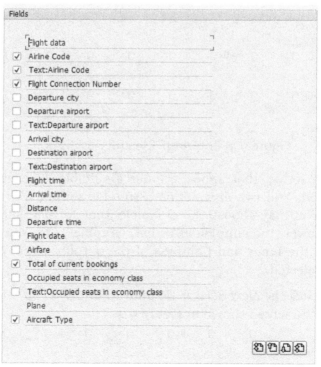

Figure 9.5: Choosing Fields

Choose the fields of your choice out of your chosen groups (you may use the *Page Up* and *Page Down* buttons to view the various fields available). In this step, you will choose all fields that you are interested in, either as a selection parameter or an output field. Once you are done, click the *Next* button. This leads you to the screen shown in Figure 9.6.

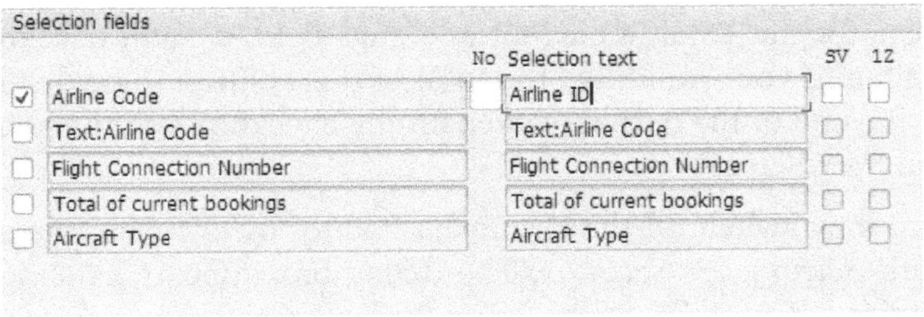

Figure 9.6: Selection Screen Fields

- The next step allows you to specify the fields that are included in the selection screen. On this screen, you will see all of the fields selected in the previous step. Use the checkbox to select the desired fields. In the example, we have chosen *Airline Code*. If you would like to change the label of the selection field on the screen, you may select the respective field using the checkbox indicator and press "Enter". The Selection text for the respective field will then be editable and you may change the text as needed. As shown in Figure 9.6, I have changed the text of the Airline Code to *Airline ID*. Once you are done with this step, click the Basic List button. This will take you to the screen shown in Figure 9.7.

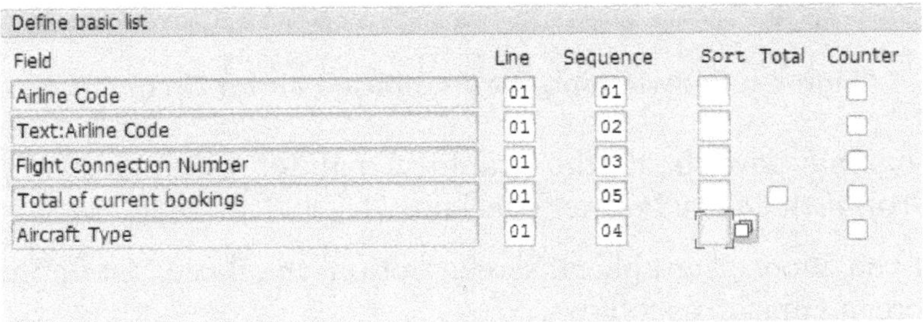

Figure 9.7: Basic List Definition Screen Without Graphical Painter

- Now you need to define the appearance of the Basic List. For single line Basic List, enter "01" in the *Line* number for all fields. For fields that you would like to define in the second line, enter "02" for the corresponding column. Moreover, you need to define the column sequence according to your requirements. I have defined the sequence shown in Figure 9.7. If you would like particular field values to be sorted, you may fill in the *Sort* field. Also, for the Total of current bookings field, a *Total* checkbox is visible. If you would like the total of this column to be displayed at the end of the output, switch on the checkbox and then choose the *Next* Screen.

You may switch off the Graphical Painter by choosing the menu path *Settings* → *Settings*. The dialog box appears as shown in Figure 9.8.

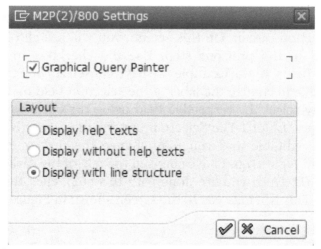

Figure 9.8: Switching the Graphical Painter On or Off

You may switch off the graphical painter by unchecking the *Graphical Query Painter* checkbox.

If you choose a graphical screen option, the Basic List definition screen appears as follows:

Figure 9.9 Basic List Definition Screen

Data fields	List fields	Selection Fields
▼ ☐ Table join	5	1
▼ ▦ Flight schedule	2	1
• Airline Code	☑	☑
• Flight Connection Number	☑	☐
• Departure city	☐	☐
• Departure airport	☐	☐
• Arrival city	☐	☐
• Destination airport	☐	☐
• Flight time	☐	☐
• Arrival time	☐	☐
• Distance	☐	☐
• Departure time	☐	☐
▼ ▦ Flight	1	0
• Flight date	☐	☐
• Airfare	☐	☐
• Total of current bookings	☑	☐
• Occupied seats in economy class	☐	☐
• Maximum capacity in economy class	☐	☐
▶ ▦ Plane	1	0
▶ ▣ Additional Fields	1	0

Figure 9.10: Left Side of Pane in Graphical View

Select the Field's checkbox to include them in the output. The preview appears on the right side of the pane as shown in Figure 9.11.

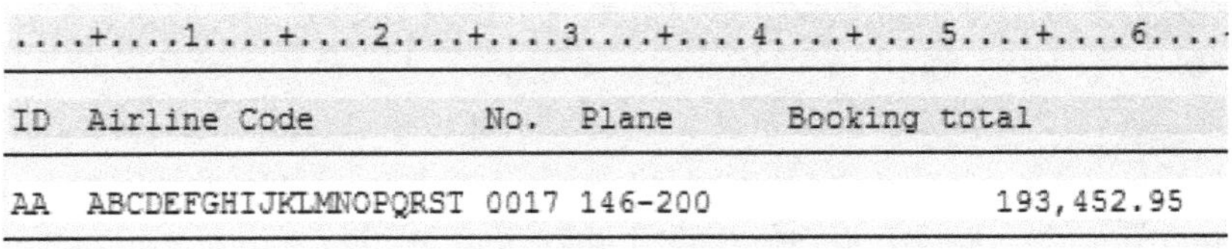

....+....1....+....2....+....3....+....4....+....5....+....6....
ID Airline Code No. Plane Booking total
AA ABCDEFGHIJKLMNOPQRST 0017 146-200 193,452.95

Figure 9.11: Report Preview

Finally, save and run your Query using the *Test* button. The screen appears as shown in Figure 9.11.

Flights Detail
Report-specific selections
Airline ID
to
Output specification
Layout

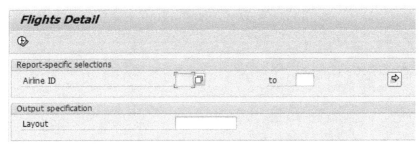

Figure 9.12: Report Selection Screen

The Query output on the chosen ALV format looks like the one shown in Figure 9.12.

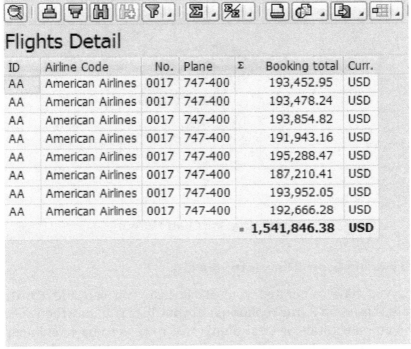

Figure 9.13: ALV Report Output With Grand Total

The ABAP list form of report for this is shown in Figure 9.14.

```
ID  Airline Code      No.  Plane        Booking total
AA  American Airlines  0017 747-400      193,452.95  USD
AA  American Airlines  0017 747-400      193,478.24  USD
AA  American Airlines  0017 747-400      193,854.82  USD
AA  American Airlines  0017 747-400      191,943.16  USD
AA  American Airlines  0017 747-400      195,288.47  USD
AA  American Airlines  0017 747-400      187,210.41  USD
AA  American Airlines  0017 747-400      193,952.05  USD
AA  American Airlines  0017 747-400      192,666.28  USD

Overall total                         1,541,846.38  USD  *
```

Figure 9.14: ABAP List Output

Also, if you have chosen a graphic output (pie chart output), it will look like the one shown in Figure 9.15.

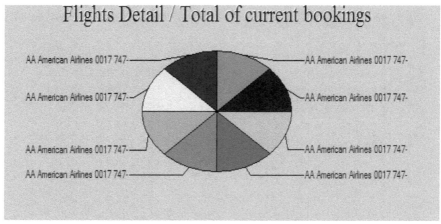

Figure 9.15: Pie Chart Output

9.2.1 Adding Control Levels to your List

Once you have generated your Basic List, you can add **Control levels** (based on Sorted columns) to your list. You may then specify if the amount totals or total number of rows is to be calculated, or whether descending sorting applicable is based for the sorted column values.

> **NOTE:** We will modify our list that was defined in the previous section to print subtotals of the bookings total of each Airline Code along with the Overall total. This will create separate totals for each airline (AA, DL, etc.).

I copied the Z_FLIGHT query that was created and named it Z_FLIGHT_CONT. An important step in defining control levels is to define the relevant field as a Sorted field in the Basic List definition. On the Basic List screen, we will specify "1" in the *Sort* field for the Airline Code as shown in Figure 9.16.

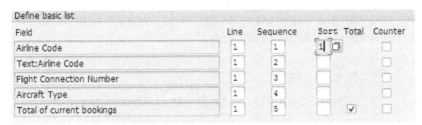

Figure 9.16: Define Basic List

Press the *Next* button, or follow the menu path *Goto* → *Basic List* → *Control Levels* (see Figure 9.17).

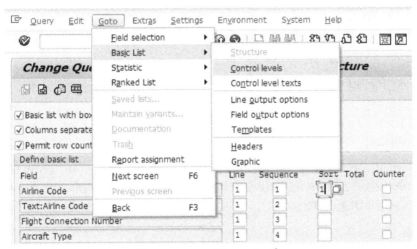

Figure 9.17: Menu Path

This will take you to the Control Levels screen, part of which is shown in Figure 9.18.

Figure 9.18: Control Levels Screen

Since our requirement is to calculate the total (or actually the subtotal) based on the Airline code, we will check the *Total* indicator as shown.

When you run the report, the output will then be shown in Figure 9.19. Each airline total is displayed.

Flights Detail

ID ▲	Airline Code	No.	Plane	Σ	Booking total	Curr.
DL	Delta Airlines	0106	A310-300		188,967.32	USD
	Delta Airlines	0106	A310-300		186,358.29	USD
	Delta Airlines	0106	A310-300		195,462.33	USD
	Delta Airlines	0106	A310-300		195,169.05	USD
	Delta Airlines	0106	A310-300		191,564.10	USD
	Delta Airlines	0106	A310-300		195,578.44	USD
DL ⌐				▪	**1,153,099.53**	**USD**

Figure 9.19: Airline Totals

9.2.2 Adding a Header and Footer to the Basic List

A useful function provided by SAP query is the ability to add headers and footers to your list. In order to add a header and footer, proceed as follows:

- On the Basic List definition screen, choose the menu path *Goto* → *Basic List* → *Headers*. The screen will then look like the one shown in Figure 9.20.

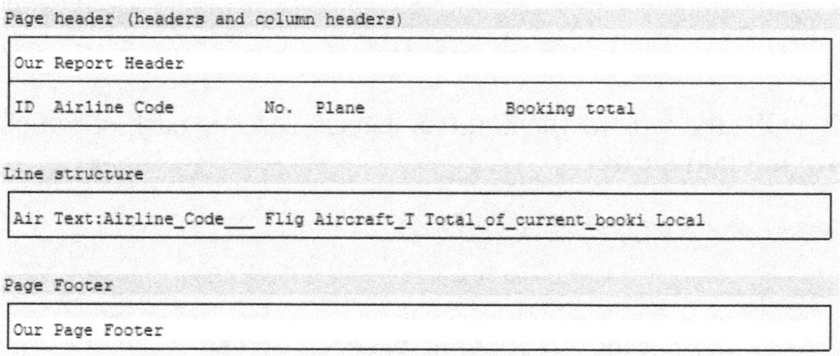

```
Page header (headers and column headers)

Our Report Header

ID  Airline Code         No.  Plane              Booking total


Line structure

Air Text:Airline_Code___ Flig Aircraft_T Total_of_current_booki Local


Page Footer

Our Page Footer
```

Figure 9.20: Adding a Header and Footer

- On top, you will find an area where we can specify the Page header (I specified it as "Our Report Header"). At the lower part of the window is an area where we can specify the Page Footer. I have specified it as "Our Page Footer".

The final output with the header and footer defined in ABAP list format is shown in Figure 9.21.

```
Our Report Header

ID  Airline Code        No.  Plane          Booking total

AA  American Airlines   0017 747-400           193,452.95  USD
AA  American Airlines   0017 747-400           193,478.24  USD
AA  American Airlines   0017 747-400           193,854.82  USD
AA  American Airlines   0017 747-400           191,943.16  USD
AA  American Airlines   0017 747-400           195,288.47  USD

Overall total                                 968,017.64  USD    *

Our Page Footer
```

Figure 9.21: Final Output with Header and Footer

To change the column header of a particular field, double-click the respective column header under the defined header of the report on the screen shown in Figure 9.20. This will open the dialog box as shown in Figure 9.22.

```
M2P(1)/800 Column Header of a Field                          [X]

Field            Total of current bookings

Heading          Income Total


Standard         Booking total
header

                                    [✓] [ Use Standard ] [✗]
```

Figure 9.22: Changing the Column Header of a Particular Field

For example, I selected the *Booking total* column as shown in Figure 9.20 and changed the column header to "Income Total" as shown in Figure 9.22.

The report will then look like the one shown in Figure 9.23.

```
Our Report Header

ID  Airline Code        No.  Plane           Income Total

AA  American Airlines   0017 747-400           193,452.95  USD
AA  American Airlines   0017 747-400           193,478.24  USD
AA  American Airlines   0017 747-400           193,854.82  USD
AA  American Airlines   0017 747-400           191,943.16  USD
AA  American Airlines   0017 747-400           195,288.47  USD

Overall total                                  968,017.64  USD   *

Our Page Footer
```

Figure 9.23: Output Report With New Column Header

Summary of Chapter 9

This chapter outlined the essentials of SAP Query for SAP users. With the information provided, you should now be able to create reports based on SAP data without the involvement of ABAP developers. You will also be able to add headers and footers as well as change the report column labels quickly and easily. Moreover, for data output that consists of amounts, quantities, or numbers, subtotals and totals may also be generated.

Chapter 10

SAP Business Workplace Part 1- Managing Documents

This chapter will focus on the SAP Business Workplace with a primary emphasis on managing documents. It will show you the range of possibilities available through the use of SAP Business Workplace and will outline the basic steps involved in accessing and using the Business Workplace efficiently. This chapter will cover the following important topics:

- *Transaction SBWP*
- *Creating a new message*
- *Using attachments*
- *Forwarding documents*
- *Creating distribution lists*
- *Working with folders and subfolders*
- *Searching within folders and subfolders*

It should be noted that within this chapter the terms document, mail and message are used interchangeably to mean any content that is sent to another user through the SAP Business Workplace. Some questions that will be answered in this chapter include:

- *How do I access the Business Workplace?*
- *How do I send mail through the Business Workplace?*
- *What is a distribution list and how is it created?*

Throughout this chapter, there will be examples and screenshots to help the reader gain the greatest possible understanding of how to utilize the SAP Business Workplace.

10.1 Overview of Transaction SBWP

The **Business Workplace** (transaction SBWP) lets you write mails (create documents), check workflows, and process work items. It is an efficient system that helps the user manage their ingoing and outgoing documents through the use of folders, subfolders, and distribution lists.

From the initial SAP screen, you may use the menu path *Menu →Business Workplace* (see Figure 10.1). Alternately, you may choose the keyboard shortcut "CTRL+F12". The direct transaction for the Workplace is SBWP.

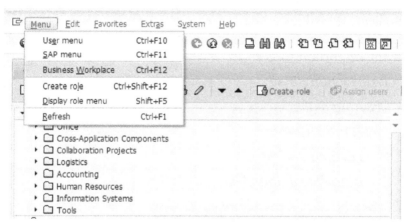

Figure 10.1: Accessing the Business Workplace

The main screen of the Business Workplace transaction is shown in Figure 10.2.

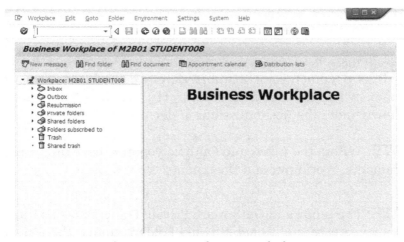

Figure 10.2: Business Workplace

The left pane shows the various folders and areas that exist, namely, **Inbox**, **Outbox**, **Resubmission**, and so on. Within the right pane there are two portions. The upper portion displays a list of items pertaining to the folder (folder node) from the left side that is selected. The list is in ALV format, and it provides an ALV toolbar that has a number of functions that may be applied to the items displayed. For more information on ALV functions, refer to chapter 6 - ALV Display Format.

The details (preview) of the selected item (for example a document) are shown in the lower part of the right pane.

> **NOTE:** There are Private and Shared Folders within the SAP Business Workplace. The Shared Folder allows you to have a central storage place where you and many other users may share or access documents and emails. On the other hand, the private folders are private to you, and no other user may access it.

Three important folders are as follows:

- *Inbox*. As the name implies, the Inbox lists the various documents (both read and unread mail) as well as workflow work items.

- *Outbox.* The Outbox lists any mail that you have sent and Workflow items executed by the user or forwarded to another user.

- *Resubmissions.* You may also resubmit workflow work items as well as documents for a future date. They will appear in the Inbox when the set date comes. The resubmitted items are shown under the Resubmissions folder.

NOTE: Within the Inbox and Outbox, you may have the Unread Documents, Workflow, and Documents.

NOTE: The Inbox and Outbox are Private Folders in your Inbox. You may create additional Private Folders under the Private Folder node.

If you need to see all of the contents of a folder, simply click that particular node. When you select *Inbox* in the left pane, you will see the contents of all the subfolders of the Inbox. If you need to view only *Unread Documents* or *Documents*, select that particular node. For example, the unread documents when selected are displayed in the right pane as shown in Figure 10.3.

Documents 14

Messag	Type	Title	Attachments	Author	Date received	↑	Copy	Resubm	Recipient
✉	📄	Error during creation of transfer		LEARN1	12/10/2009				1
✉	📄	Error during creation of transfer		LEARN1	06/03/2009				1
✉	📄	Notif. of Completion:Display mat		BC601-MGR01	04/16/2009				1
✉	📄	Notif. of Completion:Display mat		BC601-MGR01	04/16/2009				1
✉	📄	Notif. of Completion:Display mat		BC601-MGR01	04/16/2009				1
✉	📄	Notif. of Completion:Display mat		BC601-MGR01	04/16/2009				1
✉	📄	Notif. of Completion:Display mat		BC601-MGR01	04/16/2009				1
✉	📄	Notif. of Completion:Display mat		BC601-MGR01	04/16/2009				1
✉	📄	Notif. of Completion:Display mat		BC601-MGR01	04/16/2009				1
✉	📄	Notification of Absence 000000!		Workflow-System	04/13/2009				1
✉	📄	Material Analysis (PURCHIS)	📎	Jocelyn Hayes	09/26/2008				4
✉	📄	test		Jocelyn Hayes	07/25/2008				4
✉	📄	Update was terminated		LEARN1	06/01/2009		📋		1
✉	📄	Update was terminated		LEARN1	10/08/2008		📋		1

Figure 10.3: Unread Documents

From the Message symbol, you may see whether a message is Read or Unread. You will also see the Author (sender), the Date received, the title of the message, as well as the number of recipients to whom the message was sent. The Attachments 📎 symbol in the attachment column indicates whether an attachment is there or not. If you place the cursor on this symbol for a particular message, the number of attachments will be displayed.

Selecting a particular Inbox Unread or Read message will display the contents in the lower part of the right pane as shown in Figure 10.4.

Figure 10.4: Preview of A Message

You may switch the preview on or off using the *Settings → Switch Preview On/Off* option under the menu path. You may double-click a particular message to view the message or work item in a new window. A typical full-screen document display is shown in Figure 10.5.

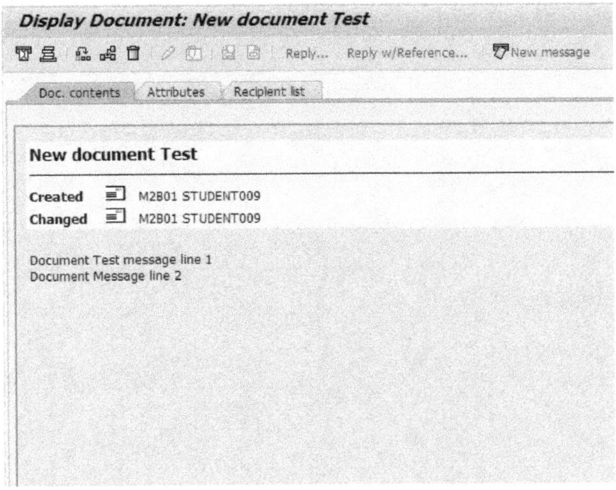

Figure 10.5: Full-Screen Document Display

As already mentioned, at the bottom of your received mail, you may have attachments in a variety of formats. For example, you may have attached files saved as Excel, Word, or text formats.

If you would like to save an attachment, first right-click the attachment, then choose the *Save As* option from the context menu that appears. Then follow the relevant steps.

10.2 Creating a New Message

Let us now see how a simple message may be created. Similar to an email message, your SAP document also has a subject, a recipient list, and a body of the email with optional attachments.

To create a new message, click the New message button on the application toolbar. The screen appears as shown in Figure 10.6.

Figure 10.6: "Create Document and Send" Screen

Enter a suitable *Title* in the field provided. A full-fledged text editor with a number of functions, such as Cut, Copy, and Paste, etc. is provided in order to fill in the text of the email.

Fill in the message text. You may also attach files to your message (we will see how this is done in the next subsection).

Once you are done, click the *Send* 🖳 button. The message that you sent will appear in the *Outbox* (under *Documents*) of the SAP Business Workplace as shown in Figure 10.7.

Figure 10.7: Message in SAP Business Workplace

In the next subsections, we will see in detail how the recipient's table may be filled in as well as the way attachments may be linked to messages.

10.2.1 Recipient Portion In Detail

As already mentioned, the recipient portion has a number of important fields. Let us see in detail the function of each field.

- *Recipient Type*. This type determines whether the document is to be sent to an SAP logon User, an Internet address, an organization, or a distribution list.

- *Recipient*. The name of the recipient. If you select the type as SAP logon Name, then you may enter an SAP user, such as LEARN1 or JONR. If you have an external address, you may enter an email address, such as abc@gmail.com. You may also specify a distribution list name. The possible values of the recipient are shown in Figure 10.8.

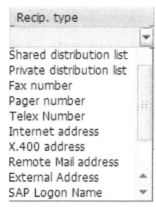

Figure 10.8: Recipient Possible Values

- *Express Checkbox.* Selecting this option displays an express message dialog box to the user telling him or her that there is an email in his inbox.

- *Copy Email Checkbox.* Checking this indicator sends a copy of the email to the desired recipient.

- *Blind Copy mail Checkbox.* Checking this indicator for a recipient will send the email as a blind carbon copy to the recipient in question.

10.2.2 Attachments

As with any email message, you may attach any document to the outgoing message. To attach a file to the email message, simply click the 📎 button on the toolbar of the *Create Document* screen.

This will show the dialog shown in Figure 10.9.

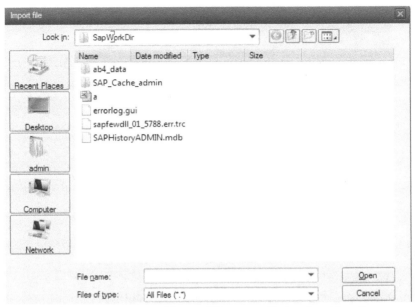

Figure 10.9: Attaching a File to an Outgoing Email

You may then browse your desktop and attach the file, such as Word, Excel, or any other format, to the message. Repeat this step for each file that you need to attach.

10.3 Forwarding Documents

You may also forward documents (you have received) to other users, provided the forwarding function is enabled on the document in question. To do this, simply select the document and right-click to access the context menu as shown in Figure 10.10.

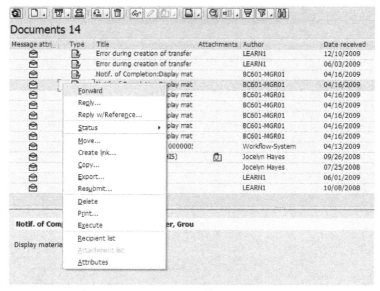

Figure 10.10 Forwarding a Document

Then choose the *Forward* option. This will display the dialog box as shown in Figure 10.11.

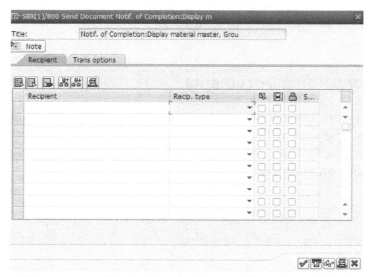

Figure 10.11: Dialog Box for Forwarding a Document

Here, you may enter the list of the recipients and the various settings as discussed earlier in section 10.2.2. When you are done, click the *Send* button.

10.4 Creating Distribution Lists

A **Distribution List** is a collection of email addresses that allows you to email multiple people at once. Instead of typing each recipient's contact information again and again, you may create a distribution list and then simply enter the name of the Distribution List as the recipient shown in Figure 10.6. A Distribution List may consist of a number of SAP addresses and users as well as external email addresses.

To create Distribution lists, click the 🔀 Distribution lists button on the toolbar. This will lead you to the screen shown in Figure 10.12.

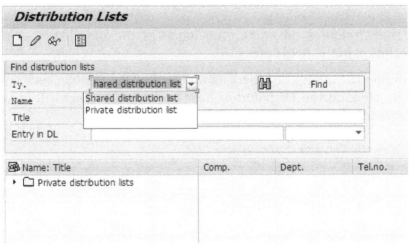

Figure 10.12: Distribution Lists Screen

This screen lets you search, display, and create lists that are both shared and private.

> **NOTE:** In addition to mass mail sending, you may also use a Distribution List in order to share a folder among various SAP users.

To create a new list, choose an appropriate list type (field with label *Ty*.). For example, choose *Private*. Then click the *Create* button. The screen appears as shown in Figure 10.13.

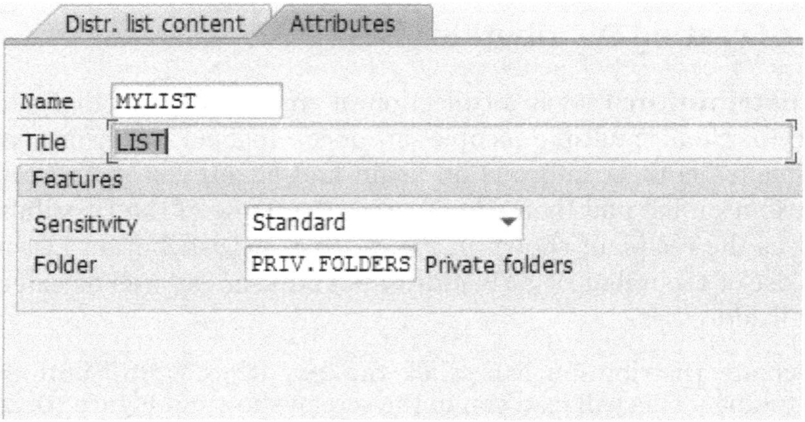

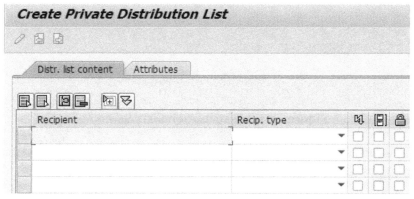

Figure 10.13: Creating A New List

On the *Attributes* tab, enter the name of the new list as a title description in the fields provided.

To define the content of the lists and listing the various recipients, simply click on the *Distribution List Content* tab. This will change the screen as shown in Figure 10.14.

Figure 10.14: Creating a Distribution List

Enter the Recipients in the spaces provided along with the Recipient type and the various options. Then click on the *Save* button.

10.5 Working with Folders and Subfolders

You may create a subfolder in the Private Folders or the Shared Folder areas. Simply select a folder. Then right-click and choose the *Create Subfolder* option.

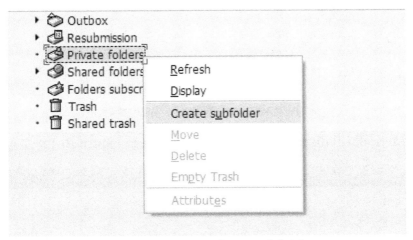

Figure 10.15: Creating a Subfolder

This action will display a screen as shown in Figure 10.16. Now you may move any document or work item into the created folder. To move a document into a folder, simply right-click the document and choose the *Move* option from the context menu.

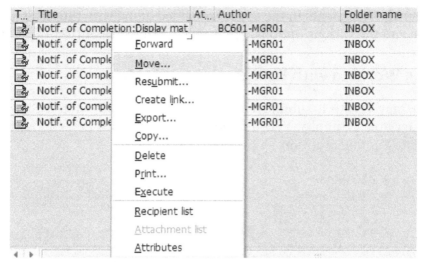

Figure 10.16: Moving a Document

This action will display the dialog box shown in Figure 10.17.

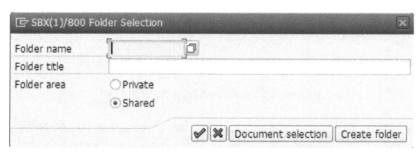

Figure 10.17: Selecting a Folder to Move

Enter the name of the folder to which you would like to move your document. The document will then shift to the specified folder.

10.6 Searching for Folders and Documents

Within the SAP Business Workplace, you may search for folders or documents quickly and easily. Let us take a closer look.

When searching for a particular folder, click the 🔡 Find folder button on the toolbar. This will display the dialog box shown in Figure 10.18.

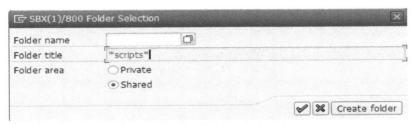

Figure 10.18: Folder Selection

You may enter either a folder name or a folder title. You also have the option of searching within the Private or Shared Folder areas. For example, if you want to search all folders that have the word "scripts" in the title, you should enter *script* in the title field as shown in Figure 10.18. The system will then show you the first folder that matches the entered search criteria as shown in Figure 10.19.

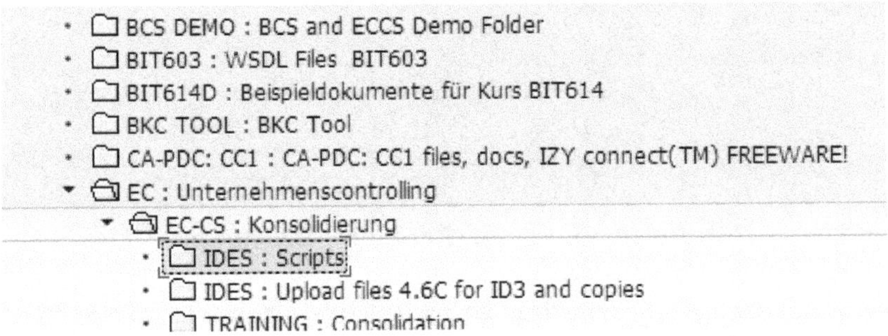

- ☐ BCS DEMO : BCS and ECCS Demo Folder
- ☐ BIT603 : WSDL Files BIT603
- ☐ BIT614D : Beispieldokumente für Kurs BIT614
- ☐ BKC TOOL : BKC Tool
- ☐ CA-PDC: CC1 : CA-PDC: CC1 files, docs, IZY connect(TM) FREEWARE!
- ▼ ☐ EC : Unternehmenscontrolling
  - ▼ ☐ EC-CS : Konsolidierung
    - · ☐ IDES : Scripts
    - · ☐ IDES : Upload files 4.6C for ID3 and copies
    - · ☐ TRAINING : Consolidation

Figure 10.19: Folder Matching Search Criteria

In addition to folders, you may also search for documents using certain search criteria. To search for documents, click the 🔲 Find document button. This will take you to the dialog box shown in Figure 10.20.

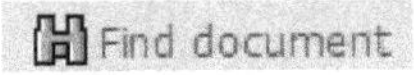

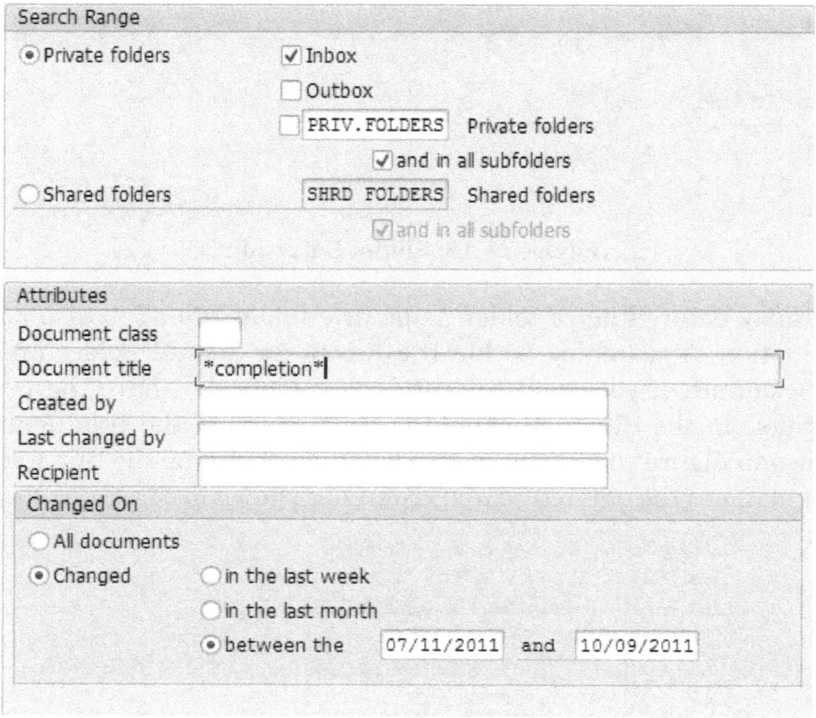

Figure 10.20: Search Range for Documents

Here, you can specify whether you want to search within the Private or Shared Folders. For the Private folders, you may specify whether you would like to search within the Inbox or Outbox, etc.

Next, enter the suitable search criteria in the *Attributes* section provided. You may, for example, specify the search string within the Document title or search by entering the creator of the document's name. You may also search for a document changed within a given date range. For example, Figure 10.20 shows the criteria entered for searching documents changed between the dates July 11, 2011 and October 9, 2011 containing the word "completion" in the document title. Once you press "Enter", the relevant documents are displayed in the top area of the right pane.

Summary of Chapter 10

This chapter discussed the SAP Business Workflow with an emphasis on creating, sending, and filing documents. With the information provided, you should now be able to access the Business Workflow, create a new message, attach documents to outgoing messages, use folders and subfolders to organize your inbox, and create distribution lists. In the next chapter, we will discuss how to manage Workflow and Work Items within the SAP Business Workplace.

Chapter 11

SAP Business Workplace Part 2- Managing Workflow Work Items

As already mentioned earlier in the book, Workflow is an important SAP functionality. Work Items are active objects that are generated during workflow execution. They are an important component of the Business Workplace, as they are executable objects that allow you to carry out different actions.

In this chapter, we will discuss what users may be required to perform with Workflow Work Items. We will discuss the various states of a Work Item and the various forms (and purposes) in which they may appear in your inbox.

This chapter will cover the following important topics:

- *How to view Work Items within your inbox and outbox*
- *How to handle a Work Item that has a deadline*
- *The various out of office settings*
- *Personalization options within the Business Workplace*

Some questions that will be answered in this chapter include:

- *How can I create and view Work Items in my inbox?*
- *What are the different statuses of Work Items?*
- *What are the applicable functions on Work Items?*

Throughout the chapter, there will be examples and screenshots to help the reader gain the greatest possible understanding of how to utilize the SAP Business Workplace.

11.1 Work Items: What They Are and How They Look

A **Work Item** is an executable object that allows you to carry out actions on business objects, such as Purchase Order, Employee absence, or Notification. In more simple terms, Work Items are generated as a result of workflow execution. They are active objects that allow you to complete an activity in the SAP system, such as an Approval work item.

Work Items appear in the Inbox of the Business Workplace mainly under the Workflow node (and a few other nodes). Your Inbox reflects all work items for which you are a recipient (or one of the recipients). A typical **Decision Work Item** is shown in Figure 11.1.

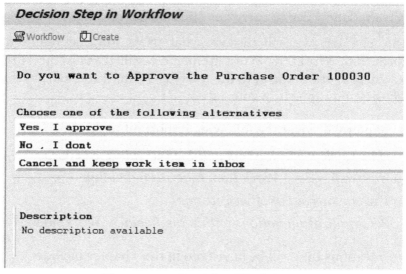

Figure 11.1: Decision Work Item

Here, you are presented with a number of choices (each of which is represented by a button) from which you can choose the option you want. You may choose the option *Yes I approve*, or *No I don't*. If you choose the *Cancel* option, the Work Item remains in your inbox for later processing. If the Yes or No options are chosen, the work item disappears from the inbox.

Other than decisions, Work Items may serve other purposes, such as:

- Work Items may be used to provide you with notification about an activity that has taken place.

- Work Items may require you to perform an action on an object in SAP transaction. In this case, you may be taken from the Work Item to the necessary transaction. Such Work Items may be required to explicitly confirm end of processing (or completion) in order for the workflow to continue further as shown in Figure 11.2.

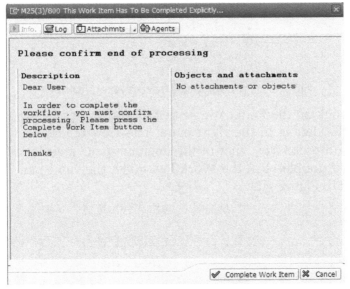

Figure 11.2: Confirm End of Processing

- Deadline Work Items/Messages for indicating that another Work Item has been overdue.

Depending on the scenario, multiple users may be involved as recipients. In this case, the Work Item may be present in the Inbox of a number of users. If one user then processes the given Work Item, the Work Item will disappear from the inbox of the other users. A Work Item may also contain attachments that may be used in the subsequent steps within the workflow in question.

11.2 Work Items View Within Inbox

Within the Inbox of your Business Workplace, there are four folders that are related to Workflow work items, namely *Workflow*, *Overdue Entries*, *Deadline Messages*, and *Incorrect Entries*.

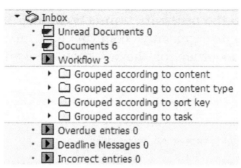

Figure 11.3: Four Workflow-related Folders

Double-click on the folder whose details you want to view. This will display the details in the right pane. The view regarding the Work Items is different from that of the documents as mentioned earlier. When you double-click the Workflow node, the right pane appears as shown in Figure 11.4.

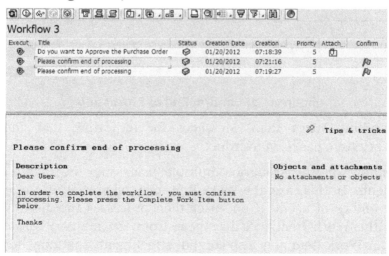

Figure 11.4: Workflow Work Items in Right Pane

The upper part shows the list of work items (also referred to as the **Work List**). At the top is a toolbar that provides a variety of useful functions that may be performed on items.

The items shown in yellow indicate Overdue Items, i.e., the items that are past their date for completion. The lower part contains the preview of the Work Item in question. This contains the description of the item and any attachments along with relevant tips and tricks. You may place the cursor on the Tips and Tricks part to fully display the Tip provided for the selected Work Item.

Within the *Object and Attachments* shown within a work item, you may click on the *Object link* to view the details of the object in consideration, such as the Purchase Order, Notification, etc.

The various columns (information) about the Work List items are shown in Figure 11.5.

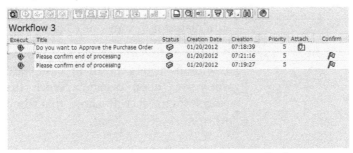

Figure 11.5: Information about the Work List Items

Let us take a detailed look:

- *Executable.* The symbol ⚙ under the Executable column for a given Work Item indicates that the Work Item may be executed. Typically, this symbol appears beside the ones for which your interaction is required.
- *Title.* This is the title (heading or subject) of the Work Item, for example, *Please Confirm End of Processing*.
- *Status.* The status shows the current state (denoted by a symbol) the Work Item is in. Some of the most important statuses (visible in the SBWP inbox) are shown in Figure 11.6.

Symbol	Status	Meaning
♢	Ready	When a Work Item initially appears in the Business Workplace, its initial state is Ready. This means that it can be executed (or processed). Also, when a Work Item is In Process status and then the Replace function is applied, it returns back to the Ready state.
♦	Executed	This is a special status for Work Items that must be explicitly confirmed. These items have been executed but not confirmed explicitly.
♠	Reserved	This indicates that you reserve that Work Item. A reserved Work Item will disappear from the inbox of other users. Once reserved, a Work Item may then be replaced by the same user or assigned by the Workflow administrator to someone else.
♢	In Process	When you execute or open a Work Item or execution, it gets the In Process status. Also, when you open decision Work Items but cancel them, it will show that they are in process.
♦	Completed	This indicates completion of the work item.

Figure 11.6: Statuses of Work Items

- *Attachment.* If an attachment for a Work Item exists, the 🗒 icon under the Attachment column will appear.

> **NOTE:** You may also sort all the items according to the column values. For example, you may sort according to the Title by clicking on *Title*. The items will be sorted according to the Title as shown in Figure 11.5.

- *Priority*. Each Work Item has a priority that indicates its urgency. This may have a range value of 1 – 9, with 1 indicating the highest priority and 9 indicating the lowest priority.

- *Confirmed Explicitly*. A flag indicator in this column for a Work Item indicates that the confirmation (completion) of the Work Item must be done explicitly, meaning the complete Work Item button will be pressed and then the workflow will proceed further.

> **NOTE:** Apart from the toolbar, you may also right-click on a particular Work Item in order to access the context menu showing the various supported functions for the select Work Item.

- *Work Item Overdue*. A Work Item may also have a latest end deadline. This is the time by which the work item will be considered late or overdue if not completed. The symbol ⏰ in this column indicates that the work item is overdue.

Over the passage of time, your Work List may become too long, and searching for a particular Work Item, a type of Work Item, or all Work Items of a particular object ID may be a challenging task. For this purpose, the Inbox view provides views of three Work Item Groupings, which are shown in Figure 11.7 (the nodes are also shown in Figure 11.2). If the user does not want to see all Work Items, he or she can view them according to the groups shown that are used to restrict the search. Selecting a particular classification with the various nodes groupings will display the items falling within the grouping in the right pane.

Work Item Groupings	Meaning
Grouped according to task	Under this node, further nodes may exist. This classification is according to the Task text, i.e., the Workflow task from which the Work Item has been generated. For example, you may have a group within the *Grouped According to Task* by the name of *Change Notification Task* or *Leave Approval Task*.
Grouped according to content	Group according to the object (with ID) in question. For example, there will be separate nodes under it, such as *Change Notification 0041* and *Change Notification 0042*. Selecting the appropriate notification will display the Work Item in the right pane.
Grouped according to content type	This grouping is based on the content type rather than the actual content. For example, there may be a node *Change Notification* which when double-clicked will display both the *Change Notification 0041* and *Change Notification 0042* in the right pane. There will be no separate nodes for the notifications 0041 and 0042 as in the Grouped by Content classification.

Figure 11.7: Work Item Groupings

11.2.1 Outbox

In the Outbox, all the workflow related items are under the *Started Workflow, Work Items Executed by me*, and *Forward Work Items*. These list any workflows started by you, the complete list of work items executed by you, and any items forwarded by you to another user, respectively.

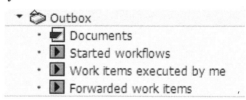

Figure 11.8: Outbox

The *Work Items Executed by me* node gives the relevant work items list. The toolbar of the Outbox also has a variety of useful functions, such as displaying of item detail, sorting, and filtering.

Work items executed by me (Since 12/26/2011)

W...	Title	Status	Executed on	Execute...
▶	Do you want to Approve the Purchase Order 100030	🔷	01/20/2012	16:01:47
▶	Do you want to Approve the Purchase Order 100034	🔷	01/20/2012	07:21:16
▶	Do you want to Approve the Purchase Order 100034	🔷	01/20/2012	07:19:27
▶	Please confirm end of processing	🔷	01/20/2012	05:38:38
▶	Do you want to Approve the Purchase Order 100034	🔷	01/20/2012	05:07:51
▶	Please confirm end of processing	🔷	01/20/2012	05:06:36
▶	Do you want to Approve the Purchase Order 100034	🔷	01/20/2012	05:05:01
▶	Please confirm end of processing	🔷	01/20/2012	05:01:45
▶	Do you want to Approve the Purchase Order 100034	🔷	01/20/2012	05:01:31
▶	Do you want to Approve the Purchase Order 100034	🔷	01/19/2012	15:35:43
▶	Do you want to Approve the Purchase Order 100034	🔷	01/19/2012	15:35:00

Figure 11.9: Work Items Executed by You

By default, the last month's items are shown. However, you may see the status of a day or week as well. For example, you may choose the 🔷 button and access the *Today Only* or the *Last 7 Days* option, whichever is required.

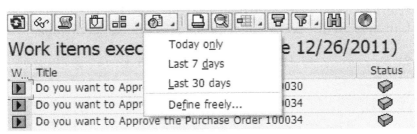

Figure 11.10: Items from Various Time Periods

11.2.2 Deadline Messages

For many Work Items, there may be a deadline set for the latest completion of the work item. Once this time has elapsed, special Deadline Messages for Work Items are issued. If you are defined as a recipient of such a message, you will receive a deadline message.

These deadline messages must be set as completed explicitly via the option *Set to Done*. When you execute the Work Item, the *Set to Done* option appears as a toolbar button (discussed in section 11.3). Also, you will find a *Monitored Work Item* button that will allow you to get information from the overdue Work Item.

> **NOTE:** Once you complete a Work Item that was sent to you and other users, it will disappear from your inbox and from the inboxes of the other users. Until they are completed, they may be in the "In Process", the "Executed", or the "Reserve" status. In all of these statuses, no other user may execute the Work Item until the "Replace" operation has been carried out.

11.3 Functions Applicable On Work Items

In this section, I will discuss the various functions that may be performed on Work Items.

- *Setting a Work Item to "Done"*. As already mentioned, for certain Work Items, including Deadline Work Items, you must explicitly confirm completion. This may be done by first selecting the relevant work item and then clicking the *Other Functions* button from the toolbar and choosing the option *Set to done*.

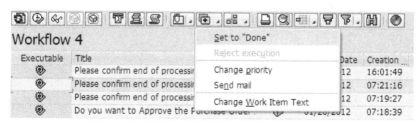

Figure 11.11: Set Work Item to "Done"

> **NOTE:** Since there is no auto-refresh in the workplace, after carrying out any function on work items, use the *Refresh* button in the toolbar to get the newest state of the Work List.

- *Creating a Link.* You may create a link to an item within a folder or a subfolder within a folder. These folders may be private or shared. To do so, select the Work Item and then choose the *Environment* ⊟ button. From the options that appear, choose *Create Link.*

Figure 11.12: Create Link

The Folder Selection dialog box appears as shown in Figure 11.13.

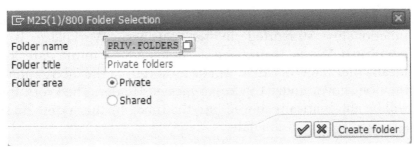

Figure 11.13: Folder Selection

You may then specify the name of the shared or private folder where the link of the Work Item is to be created.

Suppose we store it in the Private folder. After specifying the folder name as shown, the link will be created in the private folder.

- *Changing priority of a Work Item.* You may also change the priority of a Work Item (as is the case with a document). To do so, click the *Other Functions* button ⊞ after selecting the item. From the options, choose *Change Priority* option. The dialog box appears as shown in Figure 11.14.

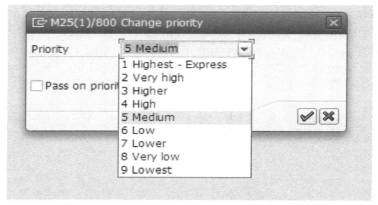

Figure 11.14: Change Priority Dialog Box

Choose the new priority of the Work Item and then press "Enter".

- *Resubmission of Work Items (and documents).* An important functionality supported in the Business Workplace is to **resubmit Work Items** and documents for a future date. This means that the Work Item will be moved from the inbox and will then be shown under the *Resubmissions* folder. The Work Item will be automatically moved into the Inbox by the system on the specified resubmission date.

Select the relevant item and click the *Resubmit* 🗐 button. (Alternately, you may right-click and choose the *Resubmit* option from the context menu.) This will display the dialog box as shown in Figure 11.15.

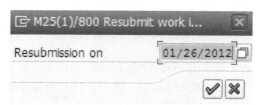

Figure 11.15: Resubmit Work Item

Then enter a suitable date when you would like the item to reappear in the Inbox. Next, press "Enter". The item will then appear in the Resubmissions folder until the date specified.

> **NOTE:** If you would like to display the Workflow log, you may select the Work Item and click the 📖 button from the toolbar.

- *Reserving a Work Item.* As already mentioned, it is possible for you to reserve a Work Item that has appeared in your inbox. Once you reserve a Work Item, it will no longer be visible to other users. Either you or the Workflow administrator can replace the Work Item manually. To reserve a Work Item, first select it and then click the *Reserve* 🔘 button. Alternately, you may right-click and then choose the *Reserve* option from the context menu.

  This will reserve the Work Item for you, and the status of the item will be changed to Reserved denoted by the ⊕ symbol.

- *Replacing a Work Item.* The Replace function sets the Work Item to Ready and makes it visible to other recipients as well for execution. This function may be applied on items that have a Reserved, In Process, or Executed status.

  To replace a Work Item, select it and then click the *Replace* 🔘 button. Alternately, you may right-click and then choose the *Replace* option from the context menu. This will replace the Work Item and the status of it will be changed to Ready ♡.

- *Adding Attachments to a Work Item.* You may also add attachments to a Work Item. You have the options of creating a new document and attaching it to the Work Item or importing an existing document stored on your PC.

  To add attachments, select the item and right-click in order to access the context menu shown in Figure 11.16.

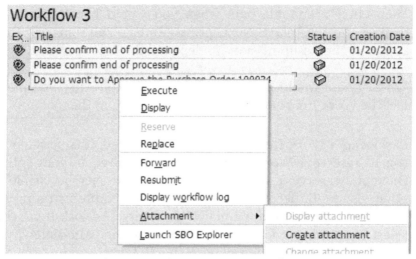

Figure 11.16: Create an Attachment

Choose the option *Create Attachment*. Alternately, you may click the 🗂 ▪ button and choose option *Create Attachment*. The dialog appears as shown in Figure 11.17.

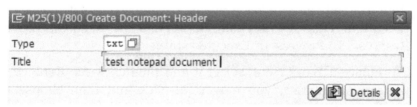

Figure 11.17: Create Document Header

NOTE: To import and attach files from your PC, click the *Import* 🔁 button and follow the steps shown.

By default, SCR appears in the Type field. The SCR denotes the text format that you may enter using the SAP editor. Suppose we choose TXT as the Type and enter a title in the provided field. When we press "Enter", a notepad document appears along with a dialog box shown in Figure 11.18.

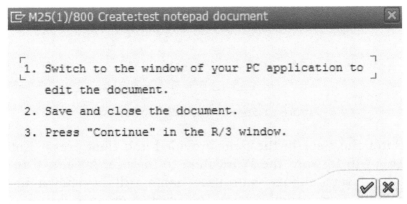

Figure 11.18: Notepad Document

You may enter the text in the text document and then save the text and close the notepad document. Next, you will need to press the *Continue* button on the dialog box shown. Once this is done, the TXT file is attached with a message saying *Attachment added to Work Item*.

NOTE: You may delete attachments that you have added, but you may not delete/remove those added by others.

The relevant Work Item's Attachment column will now appear with a 📋 symbol, denoting the presence of the attachment.

Workflow 4						
Executable	Title	Status	Creation Date	Creation	Priority	Attachments
🕸	Please confirm end of processing	⊘	01/20/2012	16:01:49	5	
🕸	Please confirm end of processing	⊘	01/20/2012	07:21:16	5	
🕸	Please confirm end of processing	⊘	01/20/2012	07:19:27	5	
🕸	Do you want to Approve the Purchase Order	⊘	01/20/2012	07:18:39	5	📋

Figure 11.19: Attachment Column

- *Forwarding Work Items.* As with documents, a Work Item may also be forwarded to any other user. This may be done by selecting the Work Item and then clicking the Forward 📧 button. Alternately, you may right-click and then choose the *Forward* option from the context menu that appears. The dialog box appears as shown in Figure 11.20.

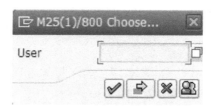

Figure 11.20: Forwarding Work Item

Enter the User in the field provided and then press "Enter". This will forward the Work Item to the user specified. In the other user's inbox, your user name will be shown in the column *Forwarded By* for the work item in question. The forwarded Work Item will be removed from all the other users' inboxes who initially had the work item visible. The item forwarded will appear in the Outbox under the node *Work Items forwarded by me.*

11.4 Out of office Settings

In this section, we will cover the steps required to set up out of office settings for when you are unable to send or receive messages. This includes creating a personal substitute and setting the forwarding option in your email.

11.4.1 Creating Substitutes

In case you are going out of office, you may allow another user (known as your **Personal Substitute**) to view your inbox and work list and approve the work items, if required. To create substitutes, choose the menu path *Settings → Workflow Settings → Maintain Substitute.* The dialog appears as shown in Figure 11.21.

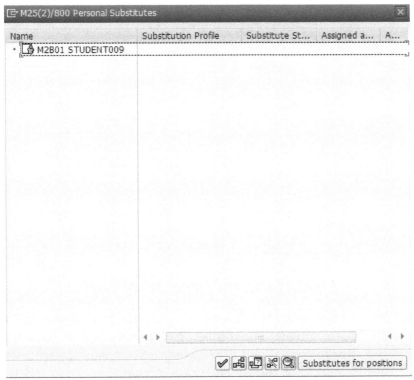

Figure 11.21: Personal Substitutes Creation

Position the cursor on your user ID (in our case, it is STUDENT009), then click the ▦ icon. A dialog box appears that will let you enter a search term for the user. In the search term field, you may either enter the name of the user or a search term. If you want to choose from all available users, you must enter the wildcard character (*). Press "Enter" to view the users selected according to the search term entered. Then choose from the list that appears.

Suppose we choose the name of the substitute to be Jane Allen. The screen appears as shown.

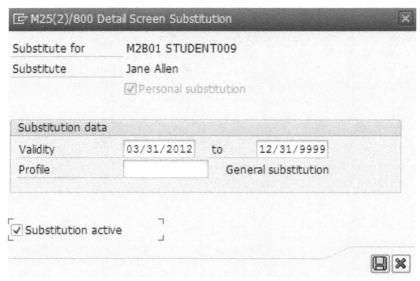

Figure 11.22: Detail Screen Substitution

Enter the validity date (duration) of the substitution as shown (it is also possible to create substitutes for a week or a month by specifying appropriate validity dates). You can activate the substitute by checking the *Substitution Active* checkbox, and then click the *Save* button.

The user Jane Allen will be one of your substitutes starting from March 31, 2012, and your work items will appear in her Inbox right away. She will remain a substitute as long as you don't delete her entry.

If the Substitution Active checkbox is not on, your substitute will have to manually adopt the substitution in order to make your work items visible in his or her Inbox. The menu option for doing so is *Settings → Workflow Settings → Adopt Substitution.*

11.4.2 Automatic Forwarding

You may also forward your documents to another SAP user or even send an email in your absence. To do this, follow the menu option *Setting → Office Settings*. This will open the Private Office Settings dialog box. Select the *Automatic Forwarding* tab and press the *Create* button. The Automatic Forwarding dialog appears as shown in Figure 11.23.

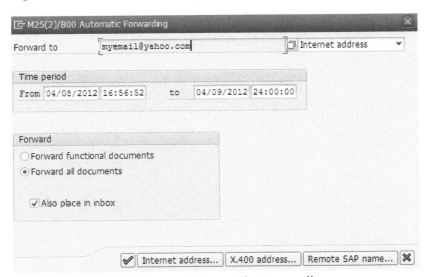

Figure 11.23: Automatic Forwarding

To forward your documents to another email address (Internet address), enter the email address in the field provided. On the right, choose the option *Internet address* from the drop box. Enter a validity period and press "Enter".

Now all documents on which forwarding is permissible will be forwarded to the specified address.

11.5 Other Personalization Options of Business Workplace

In this section, we will see some of the personalizing settings related to work items. To access this setting, choose the menu path *Settings* → *Workflow* → *Personal Settings*.

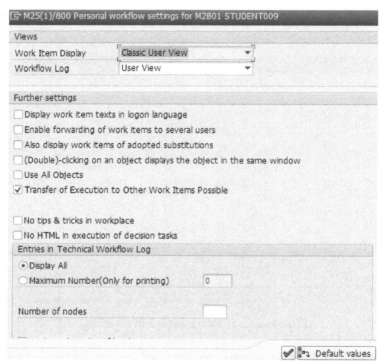

Figure 11.24: Personal Workflow Settings

A few useful settings are shown below:

- *Enable Forwarding of Work Items to Several Users.* As the name indicates, this setting allows you to forward the work item to several users. By default, this setting is switched to off.

- *No Tips and Tricks of Work Items in Workplaces.* You may switch off the Tips and Tricks displayed within a Work item by selecting this checkbox. By default this setting is on. After doing so, no tips and tricks are shown.

- *Object Details Shown in Same Window.* By default, clicking on the Object name pertaining to a particular work item opens a new window showing the details of the object. You may want to switch this off and display the object detail in the same window. You can do this by selecting the checkbox *Double-clicking object shows object in Same Window.*

> **NOTE:** If you would like to switch back the default settings of the Workplace press the ![Default values] button.

11.5.1 Switching Off Preview

You may also switch off the work item preview shown in the lower part of the right pane. You can do this by selecting the menu option, *Settings → Switch Off Preview.*

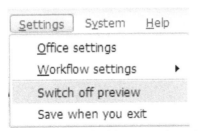

Figure 11.25: Switching Preview Off

Summary of Chapter 11

This chapter discussed the SAP Business Workflow with an emphasis on Work Items. With the information provided, you should now be able to locate Work Items within your inbox and outbox, identify deadlines on Work Items, and complete them appropriately. You should now also be comfortable with the various settings found within transaction SBWP, particularly relating to out of office settings and personalization of your Business Workplace.

Chapter 12

Miscellaneous Topics

This chapter will focus on a variety of additional topics that may be useful to the user. I will discuss in detail how to display an authorization check using Transaction SU53 and will then delve into the various functions/services pertaining to the Objects that you work with on a day-to-day basis. These miscellaneous topics are meant to help you round out your knowledge base.

The following topics will be covered:

- *Displaying Authorization Check*
- *Transaction SU53 Output*
- *Object Services*
- *Attachment Lists*
- *My Objects Lists*

Some questions that will be answered in this chapter include:

- *I cannot gain access to a transaction. What do I do?*
- *How do I display an Authorization Check?*
- *How do I alert the security team that I need access?*
- *What are the most important Object services?*
- *How do I create a note for a given Object?*

Throughout the chapter, there will be examples and screenshots to help you gain the greatest possible understanding of how to display Authorization Checks and how to manage Objects within their everyday tasks.

12.1 Transaction SU53 – Displaying Authorization Check

As already mentioned earlier in the book, the necessary authorization must be given to your User (ID) in order for you to execute a report, to make entries on a screen, or to display data through a transaction. However, there will be many situations when you should be allowed to go to a transaction or carry out a certain activity within the system but are not allowed to do so. This may also happen when you try to access a transaction via the user menu or the SAP Easy Access Menu but cannot due to lack of authorization. An authorization error displayed, in such cases, is shown in Figure 12.1.

> 🚫 You are not authorized to display users

Figure 12.1: Authorization Error

In such cases, you should ask the security team member to provide you with necessary authorization. In order to do so, you need to point out which Authorization Object check has failed. The information on the authorization object and the check that failed can be determined using **transaction SU53**.

Simply call transaction "SU53" or use menu path *System → Utilities → Display Authorization Check.*

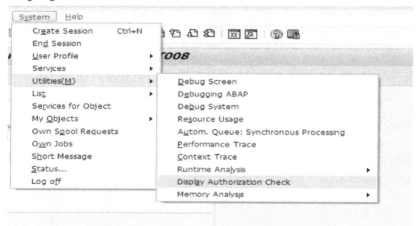

Figure 12.2: Display Authorization Check

This will take you to the Authorization Display screen. The Authorization Data shown for a check that has failed will be similar to the one shown in Figure 12.3.

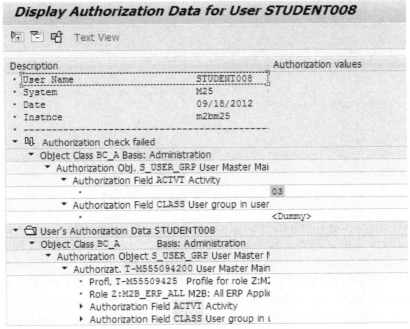

Figure 12.3: Authorization Data

It will be clearly written that the *Authority Check Failed* and the required Authorization value for the user in order to proceed with the activity will be shown in red.

You may then send this screenshot to the Security team and ask for the necessary authorization. Make sure that this SU53 screenshot is taken right after the authorization error occurs. Once the authorization is granted, you may then use the desired transaction.

> **NOTE:** It is important that you call the SU53 transaction immediately after the failing transaction.

If the last carried out check was successful, the screen appears as shown in Figure 12.4.

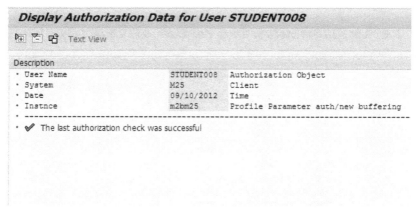

Figure 12.4: Successful Authority Check

The transaction SU53 output shows the last authorization check that was carried out by the system while the user was carrying out his or her activity (even if it was successful or not). For example, if you ran the check several hours ago, the authorization check history will still be there. However, when you log off and then again log on to the system, you will have your Authorization check history in transaction SU53 refreshed. Until the user does not log off, the outcome of the last authorization check will remain in the system.

> **NOTE:** A successful message does not require the user to do anything. The details about the generation of a failure message are what a user should send to the Security team.

12.2 Object Services

For the objects that you work with (such as a Document, a Material, or an Employee), there may be some general functions known as **Object Services** available. These may allow you to, for example, enter a note or attach a file to the object in question. This will only be relevant to the particular document number or to the particular employee to which it is attached.

To access the Object Services, click on the 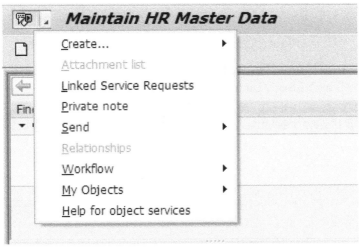 icon on the top left corner of the SAP window in order to open the submenu shown in Figure 12.5.

Figure 12.5: Object Services Submenu

The menu provides a number of options. All of these may not be applicable to your object.

Let us now look at the most important functions one by one.

- *Creating and Managing Attachments.* To create an attachment for the object in question, you may use this function. Simply choose the menu option *Create → Attachment.* The pop-up appears for specifying the file to be attached. You may then attach any file (in a number of formats, such as Word, Excel, or any other format).

  After at least one attachment (or an added note has been attached) exists for the object in question, you may display the attachments to the object by choosing the *Attachment list* option as shown in Figure 12.6.

Figure 12.6: "Attachment list" Option

The Attachment list will appear as shown in Figure 12.7. All files as well as Notes attached to the object will be shown.

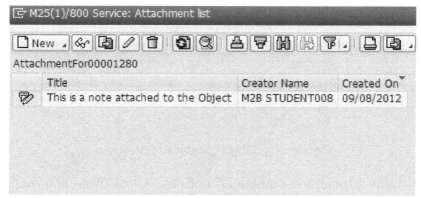

Figure 12.7: Attachment List

> **NOTE:** Private Notes do not appear in the Attachment list of the Object.

- *Create Notes (and private notes).* You may also attach notes to the given object. These may be accessible by other users (normal notes) or may be just accessible by you (**private notes**).

  To create a note for all users, choose the option *Create → Note*. The Note editor will appear as shown in Figure 12.8.

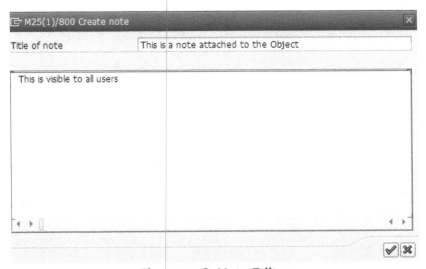

Figure 12.8: Note Editor

Enter the title of the note along with the text of the note and press "Enter".

On the other hand, to create a private Note, you should choose the option *Create → Private Note*.

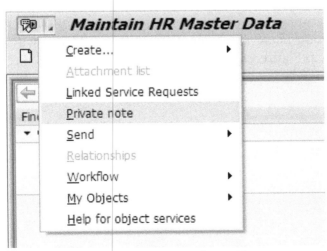

Figure 12.9: Create Private Note

This will open the Personal Note editor shown in Figure 12.10.

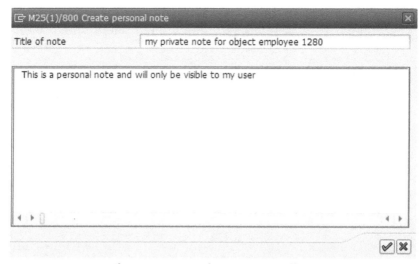

Figure 12.10: Private Note Editor

You may then enter the private note and title and press the "Enter" button.

- *Send Object with Note (in an Email).* It is also possible for you to go directly from the submenu to the Business Workplace and create an email with the link to the object attached to the email. For example, if we are processing employee 1280 and we choose the option *Send → Object With Note*, the screen will appear as shown in Figure 12.11.

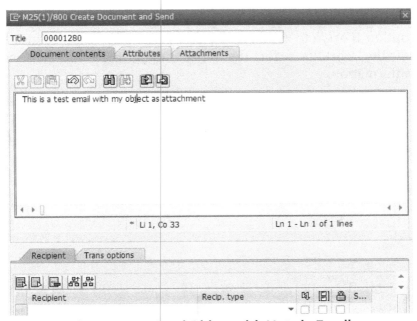

Figure 12.11: Send Object with Note in Email

We can then specify the Title, the Body of the email, and the Recipients, and then click the *Send* button. On the Attachments tab, we will see that the Employee link is attached.

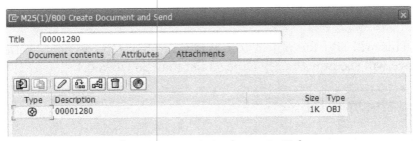

Figure 12.12: Attachments Tab

- *Starting and Displaying Workflows for an Object*. You may also have workflow functions attached that are accessible from the General Object Services. In order to start a workflow related to the object in question, simply select the menu option *Workflow → Start Workflow*.

To view a list of the workflow pertaining to the object, choose the option *Workflow* → *Workflow Overview*. This will display a list of the workflows for the object along with the necessary information.

- *Adding Object to your Favorites*. You may also add certain objects along with their IDs to your favorite Objects list. This may be done by choosing the menu option *My Objects* → *Add to My Objects*.

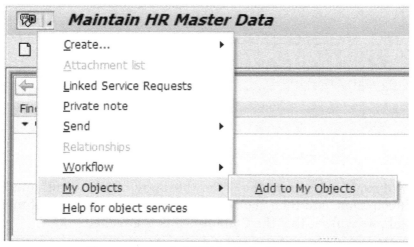

Figure 12.13: Add Objects to Favorites

This will add the object to the favorite list. (In the next section, we will see how the My Objects list may be viewed.)

12.3 The "My Objects" List

As already mentioned, there is a **My Objects** list to which you may add your favorite objects. This is particularly useful when you have certain objects that you want to note for future usage. The objects that are added to the list are not removed until you explicitly do so.

You may display, change the list, or create folders in the Objects list. To do this you may use the menu path *System* → *My Objects* → *Edit*

Objects shown in Figure 12.14. (This menu path is available in all SAP screens.)

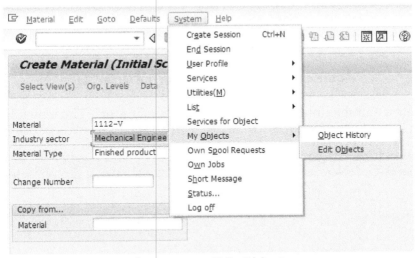

Figure 12.14: Edit Objects

The My Objects list will be displayed as shown in the Figure 12.15.

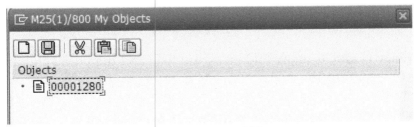

Figure 12.15: My Objects

Suppose we added the employee number 1280. A node will appear for it in the list. You may then double-click on the 1280 node and it will take you directly to the transaction for processing the given object.

You may also create folders in your favorite object list. To create a folder, click the ☐ button. The dialog appears as shown in Figure 12.16.

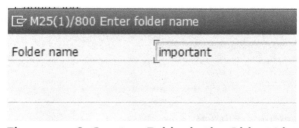

Figure 12.16: Create a Folder in the Object List

Enter a suitable folder name and then press "Enter". The new folder will be added to your list.

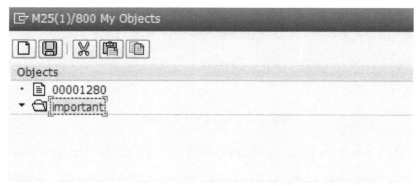

Figure 12.17: My Objects with Folder

You may create as many folders as you like, and then drag and drop any objects into the folder. To delete an object from the list or to delete the folder, select the given item and click the ✂ icon. Press the *Save* button to save your setting.

The list of objects remains and may be accessed even after you have logged off.

Summary of Chapter 12

This chapter discussed how to generate and display Authorization Checks when you are unable to access certain transactions. It also discussed different services that are available to you for Objects that are used every day. With the information provided in this chapter, you should now be able to apply the mentioned features effectively to your daily work. I hope that this information is useful to you and has helped round out your knowledge base.

References

http://help.sap.com/saphelp_erp60_sp/helpdata/en/c8/96c99814 2f11d389940000e8216438/frameset.htm

Index

As managing SAP change becomes more challenging, we keep finding ways to make it easier!

When you're facing an SAP change control problem or challenge, your approach will depend on what you know. With Salt, the unknown quickly becomes known so you can deal with it from a basis of solid knowledge.

Take 2 simple steps to see if Salt belongs in your SAP toolkit —

1. Take the Salt online Test Drive using a fully operational cloud hosted Salt installation

2. Evaluate Salt within your own SAP environment with a fully functional 90-day free trial that you can use on up to 20 SAP systems

Find out more at www.saltapps.com/testdrive-erp

Simplifying SAP change control

Author Bio

Rehan Zaidi has more than 15 years of SAP experience and has been writing about SAP topics since 2001. He is the author of the *SAP Advanced ABAP Cookbook* published from the United Kingdom, and has written a number of SAP books and articles about ABAP, Workflow, HR functional and technical consultants, and SAP user experiences. He has been published in prestigious American publications such as *SAP Professional Journal* and *HR Expert*. Rehan has provided coaching for Mobility and ABAP. He has also completed support and implementation projects for various areas of ABAP and Workflow. He holds Bachelor's and Master's degrees in computer science. Rehan can be reached at erpdomain@gmail.com.

About the Publisher

Jon Reed is an independent analyst, SAP Mentor and Enterprise Irregular who blogs and videocasts on enterprise trends. *The Ultimate SAP User Guide* is the fifth book Jon has published, and the third SAP title.

Jon's prior SAP titles are the *SAP Consultant Handbook* (1998), one of the most successful books in the SAP arena, and *The Ultimate SAP Pricing Guide*, by Matthias Liebich. The home base for Jon's SAP publishing ventures is JonERP.com, Career Answers for SAP Professionals.

Most recently, Jon is a co-founder of diginomica.com. Launched in the spring of 2013 by Jon and four other long-time enterprise bloggers, diginomica is focused on providing original commentary and reporting focused solely on the enterprise market.

Jon is also the driving force behind JonERP.com, an interactive web site for SAP professionals that features Jon's long-running podcast and video series. In his client work, Jon advises companies on enterprise go-to-market and the use of multi-media to reach new audiences. Content tactics for reaching today's informed enterprise buyer is a major focus on Jon's advisory.

The Ultimate SAP User Guide – Expert Reader Bios

*T*he *Ultimate SAP User Guide* is indebted to its expert reader panel for invaluable feedback to the final version you are reading now. Here are their bios.

Simha R. Magal, Ph.D. is Professor of Management (MIS) and Director of the ERP program in the Seidman College of Business, Grand Valley State University. Dr. Magal has taught graduate and undergraduate courses in business processes and enterprise systems using SAP for over a decade, and has coauthored three best-selling SAP books: *Essentials of Business Processes and Information Systems* (Wiley, 2009), *Integrated Business Processes with ERP* (Wiley 2012), *Business Process Integration with SAP ERP* (Epistemy Press 2013). In 2013, he co-founded Epistemy Press, a digital publisher that delivers cutting-edge SAP knowledge to both academia and industry.

In 2012, Dr. Magal was also selected by the SAP professional community to be an SAP Mentor, a rare honor for an academic. He can be reached on Twitter at: @ERPProf.

Bill Wood has deep IT experience since the mid 1980s, including over 25 SAP engagements since 1994. Wood's diverse SAP experience includes: SAP Solution Architecture, IT & business strategy integration, software & vendor selection, ITAM / SAM audits, SAP CoE development, project management, SAP project audits, methodology development, SAP upgrades, rollouts, and data conversions. Wood is ASAP certified, a former Knowledge Manager for the Grant Thornton SAP practice, and a Mensa member.

Wood runs the SAP customer centered site at R3now.com. Wood can be reached on Twitter at: @r3now.

Paul Hawking is an Associate Professor in Information Systems at Victoria University. He is considered as one of the leading commentators on ERP systems and Business Intelligence and specifically SAP solutions. His knowledge is well respected in both industry and academia and accordingly is often required to assist companies with their SAP strategies and understanding SAP solutions.

Hawking was a past Chairperson and committee member of the SAP Australian User Group (SAUG) for 10 years and was responsible for knowledge transfer. He now advises the SAUG on the content for their events. In 2009, 2011, and 2012, Hawking was voted by the SAP community as one of the Top Ten Most Influential People in SAP for Australia and New Zealand. Hawking was awarded "Outstanding Academic 2010" by SAP. He was the first academic in the world to become a SAP Mentor. Hawking can be reached on Twitter at: @paulhawking.

Leonardo De Araujo is Vice President and member of the Executive Committee at Beyond Technologies. De Araujo specializes in the implementation, optimization, support and upgrade of SAP solutions. He has over 17 years of experience as an information technology specialist. During his career, De Araujo carried out several mandates calling on his SAP solutions expertise. With his considerable technical experience and his vast business knowledge, he advises clients on the technology solutions adapted to their needs in order to maximize their profitability.

In 2009, De Araujo was named an SAP Mentor - one of the most prestigious honors in the SAP community. He regularly delivers speeches for the ASUG (America's SAP Users' Group) and the SAP TechEd conference (SAP's annual technology event now known as SAP d-code). De Araujo is based in Montréal, Québec. He can be reached on Twitter at: @Leonardo_Araujo.

Additional expert readers: Zaidi and Reed would also like to thank expert readers Nadine Baghdadi (expert SAP trainer), Rachel Meyers (expert training guide creator), and Morris Rosenthal (publishing industry expert).